Legal Almanac Series No. 46

YOUTH
AND
THE LAW

Rights, Privileges and Obligations

By
Irving J. Sloan, J.D.,

1970
OCEANA PUBLICATIONS, INC.
Dobbs Ferry, New York

This is a newly revised edition of the forty-sixth number in a series of LEGAL ALMANACS which bring you the law on various subjects in nontechnical language. These books do not take the place of your attorney's advice, but they can introduce you to your legal rights and responsibilities.

(Former edition of Legal Almanac Number 46: <u>Legal Status of Young Adults</u>, by Parnell J. T. Callahan.)

Library of Congress Catalog Card Number 77-132278

International Standard Book Number 0-379-11073-3

CONTENTS

Appendices

FOREWORD

The purpose of this small book is to give young people an opportunity to gain some measure of knowledge about their legal rights in a democratic society which strives at all times to guarantee those rights. The laws which reflect your rights are made by the representatives of the people including yourselves when you have reached voting age. If you do not like these laws you can try to elect new representatives who will change them. This power to exercise your wishes in the framing of the laws obliges you to obey them.

There are two kinds of law surveyed here. The first kind is civil law. This deals with claims for compensation for injury to a person or for damage to his property. If you are injured in an accident that is caused by the negligence of someone else, you may sue him for damages. If a person signs an agreement with you and then seeks to avoid it or in some way violates its terms, you may ask the court to make him carry out the terms of that agreement or in the alternative make him pay you money to compensate for the loss you suffered through his conduct. Civil law is used to settle disputes between individuals or groups of individuals.

The second kind of law we deal with here is criminal law. Criminal law defines what acts are illegal (stealing, for example) and what acts must be performed (such as paying income tax). It fixes a penalty for anyone who breaks its provisions. Criminal cases are prosecuted by the government so that the parties consist of public prosecutors and private individuals as defendants.

As citizens of the United States, you have certain privileges, and corresponding obligations, which vary according to your age. In some cases, there is no distinct change in your rights or obligations when you reach your "majority" (which in most states is twenty-one years). There are, however, situations where you lose certain immunities and gain certain privileges upon attaining your majority. For example, at the age of eighteen you may obtain a license to operate an automobile. No change takes place in your license as an operator upon your twenty-first birthday. On the other hand, once you reach your majority, you may sue or be sued in your own name for damages suffered by you while operating the automobile or inflicted by you on any other person. While you are a minor, whether you stand four feet four or six feet four, you may not be sued in your own name. You are also prohibited from entering most contracts, from selling or buying real estate without Court approval and without the intervention of a guardian, and from exercising even such civil rights as contracting marriage and buying alcoholic beverages.

Understand that this book is not intended to take the place of legal advice or to supplant your own or your family lawyer. There is no such thing as cheap legal advice. Throughout the Legal Almanac Series of which this is a part, you are reminded that there is nothing and no one to take the place of a qualified legal advisor who is a member of the bar of your state of residence. This book may very well raise some issues concerning your legal responsibilities or the rights extended to you by the laws of your own State, and under such circumstances you should indeed consult your attorney.

Our laws, and the procedures for implementing them, safeguard our liberties. Observing the laws, and exercising democratic processes to change them if and when necessary, is the best way to further progress in our essentially free society. Beyond that, from your own personal point of view, you must conduct your life to avoid any criminal record or civil judgment. In other words, avoid making a record for yourself so that you can begin your adult life and career unburdened by "indiscretions" of youth which the law itself penalizes.

Chapter One
YOUTH AND CITIZENSHIP

Citizenship and the Constitutions

The Fourteenth Amendment of the United States Constitution provides that, "All persons born or naturalized in the United States and subject to the jurisdiction thereof, are citizens of the United States and the state wherein they reside." This is the only definition of citizenship in the Constitution. For all Americans, it means that because they live in the United States they are subject to and must obey its laws. But it does not specifically describe the relationship between citizens and the government, the rights and duties of the ruled and the ruler.

Interpreting the Fourteenth Amendment, the United States Supreme Court explained the relationship in this way:

"There cannot be a nation without people. The very idea of a political community such as a nation is, implies an association of persons for the promotion of the common welfare. Each one of the persons associated becomes a member of the nation formed by the association. He owes it allegiance and is entitled to its protection. Allegiance and protection are, in this connection, reciprocal obligations. The one is compensation for the other: allegiance for protection and protection for allegiance." 𝟛

This means, simply, that citizens and their government work together, each receiving benefits and giving services. The government (on every level: city, county, state, federal) is established to serve the needs of the people by making new laws and to provide order by enforcing existing laws. On the other hand, the people have the right to seek changes in the law by choosing and changing the men in the government who make and enforce law. Such change is achieved by exercising the right to vote.

Registration and Voting

Theoretically, every adult American citizen may vote in the United States. Actually, apart from Presidential elections much less than half of the eligible voters participate in the electoral process and even in such Presidential elections not much more than half of the voting population exercises this all-important right.

Most states' voting requirements are very similar. Generally, they give the vote to all citizens, men and women, who have reached twenty-one years of age and have lived in the state a year and in the county or voting district for two or three months. Usually the states do not allow prisoners and the mentally ill to vote. In some states certain criminals, even though they have served their term, lose their voting rights forever.

Seventeen states provide that voters must pass literacy tests to prove they can read and write (more recent court cases have held that literacy can be in any language, not just English). Seven require voters to take an oath of loyalty to the Constitution. All the states have systems of registration whereby potential voters must prove their voting eligibility within a stated number of days before election. The local registrar of voters or the county clerk can give you registration and voting requirements in your own state.

The minimum voting age has become a major issue in recent years. This is an important question for young men and women who are now in high school.

A few states have lowered the voting age to eighteen, nineteen or twenty--below the twenty-one years old standard which has always prevailed in a vast majority of the states. The President's Commission on Registration and Voting Participation recommended in November, 1963, that the minimum voting age of eighteen should be considered by states. In 1970 Congress passed federal legislation which would accomplish this proposal. There is, however, a constitutional question involved whether Congress can establish such a voting requirement for all states for all elections, state and local as well as federal offices. While the President of the United States signed the legislation he expressed doubts about the constitutionality of it. At the time of publication of this book the issue had not been resolved in the courts. It is strongly believed, nevertheless, that if the legislation should fail to pass the constitutional elements in the courts it will relatively quickly be passed as an Amendment to the Constitution even before the Presidential elections of 1972.

Minority and Majority

Although certain privileges are extended to minors at varying ages in different states, the conferring of these privileges does not permit you to exercise all the rights of citizenship. While the rights are there, and belong to you, you may not exercise those rights until you actually attain the given age specified in your particular state.

You attain a given age not on your birthday but on the day before the birthdate. This is not only important in determining your right to vote, it is also important in the determination of your civil rights and obligations. Thus the age at which you may make a valid Last Will and Testament varies from state to state, and you may exercise that right on the day before your birthday. By the same token, an act committed on one day may be juvenile delinquency, while a day later it may be a felony, punishable by confinement in state prison.

Chapter Two
YOUTH AND SELECTIVE SERVICE

The Selective Service System was created to provide an orderly method of registering the young men of the nation and classifying them as to their availability for military service from the viewpoint of the national health, safety, or interest.

When you register on your eighteenth birthday with the Local Board you sign up for military service if you are needed. Every young man has this duty. But you also have certain rights that you can use to help your Local Board decide when you should serve.

If the Armed Services need many men your chances of being called will be greater. When military needs are low, the chances of your being called will be less. The Department of Defense determines how many are needed to serve.

It is a privilege to serve in the Armed Forces of the United States. Most of the men now in the Armed Forces volunteered. Since not enough volunteer, however, local Draft Boards must make up the difference.

Random Selection for Military Service

The Military Selective Service Act of 1967 was amended on November 26, 1969, to authorize the President to implement a system of random selection for military service. Acting under that authority, the President issued Proclamation No. 3945 establishing such a system.

The random selection sequence was initiated on December 1, 1969, by drawing 366 dates of birth (month and day only). This applied to all registrants 19 but not 26 years of age as of December 21, 1969. The sequence of the drawing of a date of birth determined the random sequence number for selection for induction. For example, September 14 was the first birth date drawn, and all registrants included in the drawing with that date of birth were as-

4

signed random sequence number 1; April 24 was the second date of birth drawn, so registrants with that birth date became random sequence number 2; and the last date drawn was June 8 and those registrants were assigned random sequence number 366. The random sequence numbers assigned are permanent. The second lottery was held on July 1, 1970, affecting only men born in 1951 whose 19th birthday is in 1970. It is planned that each year a drawing will be conducted for the purpose of assigning random sequence numbers to those registrants who attain the 19th anniversary of their dates of birth during that calendar year. These numbers are also permanent for the registrants included in that drawing.

A registrant with a deferment would not be subject to call while deferred. However, when his deferment expires and he is placed in Class I-A or I-A-O, he would be subject to call with the age group then being called in accordance with the random sequence number initially assigned to him. Any registrant classified in Class I-A or Class I-A-O who is subject to random selection, whose random sequence number has been reached, and who would have been ordered to report for induction except for delays due to a pending personal appearance, appeal, preinduction examination, reclassification, or otherwise, shall, if and when found acceptable and when such delay is concluded, be ordered to report for induction next after delinquents and volunteers even if the year in which he otherwise would have been selected has ended and even if (in cases of extended liability) he has attained his 26th birthday.

Every registrant is classified on an individual basis. Blanket deferments are prohibited by law. Deferments are reviewed at least once each year but every classification will be reconsidered when there is a change in the conditions upon which the classification is based.

A registrant has the right to request a personal appearance before his board within 30 days of the date of mailing of any notice of classification by the local board. Following such personal appearance, he will be given a new classification card, and will have the right to appeal that classification within 30 days. A personal appearance before the local board is not required, and any registrant may bypass this step and make a direct request for appeal.

Along with the Classification Notice mailed to registrants classified in Classes I-A, I-A-O and I-O, there will be forwarded

5

information that a Government Appeal Agent is available to them for legal advice on Selective Service matters, particularly in connection with appeals.

Registrants who qualify for deferment may appeal for a change in classification to II-S (student) or II-A (occupational) classifications within 30 days of the date of mailing of a notice of classification. Requests for appeal should be sent to the registrant's local board, and should be accompanied by supporting letters and documents from teachers, employers, dependents, or others to justify the registrant's claim.

A registrant has the right to request a transfer of his appeal to the appeal board having jurisdiction over his principal place of employment or place of residence, if his local board is in a different state or jurisdictional area. The request for transfer must be made at the same time that the appeal is requested. The local board will forward the entire file to the appeal board, which may change or sustain the classification given the registrant.

Denial of deferment at the state level may be appealed to the President within 30 days if the vote of the appeal board was split. If the vote was unanimous, the registrant, an employer, a school, or a disinterested agency such as the Scientific Manpower Commission, may seek review at the State Selective Service Headquarters and following that review, may seek further review at National Selective Service Headquarters in Washington, D.C. The State Director in the local board state, the State director in the appeal board state, or the National Director of Selective Service may take an appeal to the President following unanimous classification by the appeal board.

A registrant cannot be inducted during the time any appeal is pending.

No deferment is valid for a period longer than one year. However, most deferments may be renewed. The registrant and his employer or his school should apply for a continuation of the deferred classification prior to its expiration. The registrant is responsible for keeping his local board up-to-date on his status. In the case of students, the request for continued deferment should be made on Form 104 and must be supported by Form 103 or 109, or any revised versions thereof that may be issued.

When a classification is re-opened and considered anew by

the local board, rights of appeal are re-established. No local board may deny an appeal.

Registrants who have passed their 26th birthday without fulfilling their military obligation are dropped next to the bottom of the call list. Registrants deferred under authority of regulations issued by the President remain liable for service until they are 35 years old.

Most Selective Service troubles arise because of (a) the registrant's ignorance of, or carelessness about, his rights, expecially the right of appealing any new classification given by the local board; and (b) the registrant's failure to keep his local board informed of changes in status, qualification, and location. Correction rests with the registrant.

High School Students

The full-time, satisfactory high school student who is ordered for induction shall be deferred in Class I-S. This deferment classification ends when he graduates or reaches age 20 or ceases satisfactorily to pursue a full-time course of study. The student seeking this deferment should ask the school principal to write to the local board giving the pertinent information.

Undergraduates

Presidential regulations provide that any undergraduate student who is satisfactorily pursuing a full-time course of instruction at a college or university shall be deferred at his request until he completes his baccalaureate degree, fails to pursue satisfactorily a full-time course of study, or attains the age of 24, whichever occurs first. The student must request such deferment in order to be placed in Class II-S, and in so doing he forfeits his right to deferment for fatherhood after completing his education, unless his induction would create a hardship for his dependents.

Additionally, until his thirty-fifth birthday, he shall be subject to call in the prime age group if calls are placed by age group and if he ceases to be in a deferred class. However, he is not restricted from occupational deferment because he has been deferred as a student. The request for student deferment should be made on SSS Form 104 if available, but may be in the form of a letter requesting deferment.

The student must provide his local board each year with evidence that he is satisfactorily pursuing his full-time course of study.

The undergraduate student who elects not to request student deferment, and who is ordered for induction during a school year, shall be placed in Class I-S (C) if he is satisfactorily pursuing full-time instruction at a college, university, or similar institution of learning, provided he had not previously béen placed in Class I-S (C). He will be retained in this classification until the end of his academic year, or until he ceases satisfactorily to pursue such course of instruction, whichever is eariler.

A student's academic year includes the 12-month period following the beginning of his course of study or its anniversary.

A full-time course of instruction requires that the student earn within one calendar year a sufficient number of credits to represent a direct proportion of his total required number of credits. For example, a student in a four-year baccalaureate course should have earned one-fourth of the credits required for his degree at the end of his first academic year, half at the end of his second academic year, and three-fourths at the end of his third academic year.

Graduate Students

A student shall be placed in Class II-S if he is satisfactorily pursuing a course of graduate study in medicine, dentistry, veterinary medicine, osteopathy, or such other subjects necessary to the maintenance of the national health, safety, or interest as are identified by the Director of Selective Service upon advice of the National Security Council.

ROTC Students

ROTC students are deferred in Class I-D until completion of college work. There is no such thing as permanent deferment or exemption from service for ROTC graduates, except under conditions of extreme personal or community hardship which cannot be alleviated by temporary delay.

Reservists

There are two branches of the Reserve--the Ready Reserve and the Standby Reserve. The Ready Reserve may be called up on very short notice. Generally, Standby reservists would be called up only after all Ready Reserve Units were called.

A registrant may enlist in a Reserve unit at any time prior to the issuance of orders for him to report for induction, or prior to his scheduled date of induction if a determination has been made by the Governor of the state (for the National Guard) or the President (for the Regular Reserve) that the strength of the Ready Reserve cannot be maintained by the enlistment or appointment of persons who have not been issued orders to report for induction. A reservist shall be classified in I-D and shall remain eligible for that classification so long as he serves satisfactorily as a member of an organized unit of the Ready Reserve or the National Guard.

Present regulations provide for the classifications enumerated below in Table I.

TABLE I

SELECTIVE SERVICE CLASSIFICATIONS

Class I-A: Available for military service.

Class I-A-O: Conscientious objector available for non-combatant military service only.

Class I-C: Member of the Armed Forces of the United States, the Environmental Science Services Administration or the Public Health Service.

Class I-D: Member of reserve component or student taking military training.

Class I-O: Conscientious objector available for civilian

9

TABLE I (continued)

Class I-O: (continued)	work contributing to the maintenance of the national health, safety, or interest.
Class I-S:	Student deferred by statute.
Class I-Y:	Registrant qualified for military service only in event of war or national emergency.
Class I-W:	Conscientious objector performing civilian work contributing to the maintenance of the national health, safety, or interest.
Class II-A:	Registrant deferred because of civilian occupation (except agriculture and activity in study).
Class II-C:	Registrant deferred because of agricultural occupation.
Class II-S:	Registrant deferred because of activity in study.
Class III-A:	Registrant with a child or children; and registrant deferred by reason of extreme hardship of dependents.
Class IV-A:	Registrant who had completed service; sole surviving son.
Class IV-B:	Official deferred by law.
Class IV-C:	Alien deferred by law.
Class IV-D:	Minister of religion or divinity student.
Class IV-F:	Registrant not qualified for any military service.
Class V-A:	Registrant over the age of liability for military service.

Americans have historically respected those fellow Americans whose moral convictions forbid them to bear arms against others. But when it comes to military conscription the legal question is how to establish a standard that exempts only sincere conscientious objectors--not men who merely seek to avoid their duty under the Selective Service System.

In World War I, the Selective Service System law exempted from combat only members of organized church groups which made the bearing of arms a religious tenet so that to do so would be in violation of that religion. The Quakers were the best-known example of this. But since World War II the requirement of formal religious beliefs and practices have been increasingly challenged. In 1965 the Supreme Court ruled that objectors need not believe in a "Supreme Being," but left open the question about what constitutes religious belief. In 1970 the Court ruled that exemption can be based solely on moral and ethical grounds. Noting that the draft law bars exemption based on "essentially political, sociological or philosophical views, or a merely moral code," the Court went on to suggest that such views can be held so firmly as to be "religious" in the eyes of the law. Because few registrants know how broadly the law defines that word, the Court said, their statements that their beliefs are nonreligious are "highly unreliable." According to this case, the law actually exempts "all those whose consciences, spurred by deeply held moral, ethical, or religious beliefs, would give them no rest or peace if they allowed themselves to become part of an instrument of war."

A great deal of controversy has risen from this decision and the law at this point is probably in a state of flux. Draft boards have been given the following guidelines stating that every applicant for Conscientious Objector status must:

(1) Be sincere in his beliefs.

(2) Be opposed to war in all forms.

(3) Be possessed of beliefs that are more than a personal moral code: he must have taken into account the "thoughts of wise men" and consulted some system of belief beyond his own personal interest, desire, or wishes on the question.

(4) Have arrived at his beliefs after "some kind of rigorous

religious training."

It is strongly urged that our readers consult the most current rules and regulations concerning this issue of Conscientious Objectors should this be a basis of their appeal from military service.

Chapter Three

YOUTH AND THE SCHOOL

Every state in the United States has on its statute books a compulsory education law. This means that young people between stated ages, which is somewhat different in different states, must attend school. But in the enactment and enforcement of such compulsory attendance legislation there is an attempt to strike a balance between the rights of the individual and those of the State. Enforcement of this law must always be reasonable. For example, if a child is ill, lives an unreasonable distance from school and transportation and transportation is not furnished, or there are other good reasons for failure to attend school, he is not a truant and his parents are not guilty of keeping him out of school in violation of the law.

Many states permit instruction of pupils outside the schools. In some cases a tutor is employed or the parents assume the obligation of teaching their children. When, however, such legal permission is granted, it must be carried out in good faith and not as a way of covering up an attempt to avoid sending the children to school. Generally speaking, attendance at schools is required and private teaching situations are rarely approved.

Residence for School Purposes

While the right of pupils to attend school in particular districts depends upon the wording of the statute, it is usually provided that they may attend the schools of the district in which they reside without payment of tuition. What constitutes residence for school purposes is not easy to determine in many cases, and the problem is frequently brought to court. The general rule is that the legal residence of a minor child is that of his father and he is legally incapable of establishing another residence in the

13

absence of special circumstances, such as the death of the father, the case of separation of the parents when the mother is given custody of the child, or a situation where other persons have the legal custody of the child. The test of the right to free attendance depends upon whether the residence is established primarily for school purposes, and whether it is intended to move from the district as soon as the benefits have been achieved.

Expulsion and Suspension of Pupils in General

The power to make reasonable rules and regulations for the conduct of the schools is delegated to boards of education by specific legislation, or is held to be implied, and pupils may be suspended or expelled for the violation of reasonable rules. In some cases the reasonableness of rules is obvious, but in the majority of situations there is no certainty about how the courts will hold in particular cases. The general principle is that if pupil conduct is such as to satisfy the school authorities that the presence of the pupil is detrimental to the best interests of the school, he may be expelled or suspended even though there is no express rule against the particular conduct complained of.

Student Rights

In recent years there has been an increasing number of cases dealing with student activism and student rights. Such cases involve matters of appearance (dress, haircuts, sideburns, and beards) and matters of free expression in connection with student publications as well as student demonstrations, wearing symbolic buttons, armbands, et al.

The present desire of high school students for longer hair prompted many schools to establish rules limiting the length that male students could wear their hair. These rules resulted in court suits by suspended or expelled students.

Until recent times the judicial view of hair and beards was that mere expectation of disruption of the learning process was sufficient justification for a regulation. Now the courts dealing with such cases require greater justification for the adoption of a regulation.

In one case, three members of a rock and roll group, who

14

were required by a contract to have "Beatle" haircuts, were refused admission to the local high school. In arguing before the federal court, the students categorized the length and style of their hair as a form of expression, similar to thought and speech, which would be constitutionally protected. There had been some testimony that students with long hair created problems in the classroom, which made the rule, according to the federal court, reasonable, and not an unreasonable regulation on the part of the school authorities. The court ruled that the constitutional rights of the students were not violated. In so deciding, the court said that the interest of the state in maintaining an orderly system of education was of first importance and the decision of the principal not to admit the students was upheld.

On the other hand, other cases resulted in favorable decisions for the students. In one case, a federal district court held that a regulation of the board of education which prohibited long hair, sideburns, and beards was unconstitutional. Two senior high school students had been expelled for violating this regulation. The court believed that without serious justification, long hair was a freedom that the state could not regulate. In finding no justification for the regulation, the court observed that there was no direct testimony that the students had been a distraction in the classroom, nor any evidence that the academic performance of male students with long hair was inferior to that of male students with short hair. The boys were allowed to keep their long hair, and their reinstatement was ordered.

Another decision in favor of the student came about because of the vagueness of a high school handbook regulation which stated that "extremes of hair style are not acceptable." The vice-principal had determined that a student's hair was an extreme style, and the student was therefore suspended from the school. The student was never told exactly what constituted an extreme style or how much of a haircut would produce an acceptable style. The court found that the regulation was unconstitutionally vague and the student was ordered reinstated. However, the court did state that where there is clear evidence "that an aspect of a student's dress or appearance has a disruptive effect within a school, the board may prohibit it."

It is apparent, then, that where in a particular school setting or situation it can be shown by the school authorities that the learning climate of the classroom or the school as a whole is in fact being disrupted by the presence of students wearing a hair style or even outer clothing of extravagant color or styling, such authorities can order the removal of such students from the school. But as this kind of grooming or clothing increases among students so that it is no longer unusual and therefore not distracting even to those who do not themselves adopt the "style," the factor of disruption becomes less significant. Without this factor the courts are not likely to uphold such restrictions on student appearance and dress.

Another set of cases on student rights deal with printed material, either in the possession of or published by students. In a recent decision, an eleventh-grade student was expelled for violating a school directive prohibiting possession of obscene literature. The principal found that the material in question was obscene because of the presence of certain words. The presence of these words was the only reason for the action taken. However, the objectionable words were also found in a novel that was required reading for the student and in a magazine that was in the school library. The federal court upheld the validity of the regulation as being in the area of "speech or action that intrudes upon the work of the school or the rights of other students."

In another case a high school student was suspended when he refused to surrender copies of a newspaper entitled High School Free Press to the principal and advised another student to likewise refuse to hand over his copies. The student had previously been informed that he would not be permitted to distribute the material on school grounds. Following his suspension, the student subsequently reappeared in the classroom without permission. In court, the student contended that he had been unconstitutionally punished for the exercise of his First Amendment rights. The court said that the student's total conduct went beyond the right to disseminate a subterranean paper but rather exhibited a pattern of open and flagrant disrespect and contempt for the officials of the school. The court concluded by saying that freedom of speech is not an absolute and the First Amendment rights of the student must be balanced against the duty and obligation of the state to educate students in an orderly manner and to protect the rights of all the students in the system. The court refused to rule against the suspension.

It does seem that at the present time the courts are rather generous in supporting the school authorities. Limitations upon how far students may go in the use of obscene language ("obscenity" in itself has defied definition even when courts have attempted to deal with it) and in criticising school personnel and school policies.

The American Civil Liberties Union, however, has offered the following set of principles dealing with student publications which the courts may or may not eventually follow to varying degrees in protecting student rights in this area:

"Generally speaking, students should be permitted and encouraged to produce such publications as they wish. Faculty advisors should serve as consultants on format and suitability of the materials, but neither they nor the principal should prohibit the publication or distribution of material except when the health and safety of students or the educational process are threatened, or the material might be of a libelous nature. Such judgment, however, should never be exercised because of disapproval or disagreement with the article in question.

"The administration and faculty should ensure that students and faculty may have their views represented in the school newspaper, and where feasible, should permit multiple and competing periodicals, perhaps produced by existing groups or by individuals banded together for this purpose."

The most significant statement of the Supreme Court of the United States on the rights and privileges of secondary school students in recent times was handed down in 1969 in a case dealing with the wearing of black armbands as an expression of protest against the Vietnam war. This case will be a landmark for the guidance of both federal and state courts for some time to come. Here the school officials became aware of a planned protest against the Vietnam conflict and adopted a policy to the effect that any student who wore a black armband to school and refused to remove it when asked, would be suspended. Five students were suspended when they took part in this silent protest against the war in Vietnam. After the planned period of protest the students were readmitted to school. They then sought an injunction in federal district court restraining the school officials from disciplining them and also sought nominal damages. The court held that the action of the school was reasonable in order to prevent disturbance of school discipline. The U.S. Court of Appeals upheld the decision on appeal by the students. The Supreme Court of the United States ruled that the problem was one of "pure speech," and stated that the case did not concern speech or action that intruded upon the work of the school or the rights of other students. The Supreme Court did not agree with the lower court, the District Court, that the regulation was reasonable because it was based upon fear of a disturbance and said that "undifferentiated fear or apprehension is not enough to overcome the right to freedom of expression." It appeared to the Court that the school authorities had "an urgent wish to avoid any controversy which might result from the expression, even by the silent symbol of armbands, of opposition to this Nation's part in the conflagration in Vietnam." The authorities had picked out a particular symbol--black armbands--to prohibit while permitting other symbols to be worn. The Court ruled that the students had the right to express their opinion in the form they did since they neither disrupted school activities nor sought to intrude in the school affairs or in the lives of others. The Court spoke of the rights of students in these words:

> "School officials do not possess absolute authority over their students. Students in school as well as out of school are 'persons' under our Constitution. They are possessed of fundamental rights which the State must respect, just as they themselves must respect their obligations to the State. In our system, students may not be regarded as closed-circuit recipients of only that which the State chooses to communicate. They may not be confined to the expression of those sentiments that are officially approved. In the absence of a specific showing of constitutionally valid reasons to regulate their speech, students are entitled to freedom of expression of their views."

It thus appears that the central issue in the area of student rights is disruption. As pointed out in the above Supreme Court case, the mere fear or apprehension on the part of school officials that a disruption will occur is not sufficient justification

18

for a regulation that infringes upon the First Amendment rights of a student. Attendance at a public school is not an automatic waiver of a student's constitutional rights. Regulations for their own sake do not appear to be acceptable by the courts. If the long hair, beard, armband, or publication does not upset the order of the classroom or impinge upon the freedom of other students, the student is likely to prevail in court. The school district must be careful to balance out the rights of the student against the order of the classroom.

Apart from the substantive rights of students which we have been dealing with thus far in this discussion of student rights, there is the equally important matter of procedural rights. Here we are concerned with "due process"--the right to be heard in a fair trial of the charges made against a student which results in his suspension or expulsion from school. It is now firmly established that before students at a tax-supported institution of learning can be expelled or given a lengthy suspension for misconduct, they must be given notice of the charges against them and some type of hearing that will at least comport with minimum due process standards.

Many of the issues yet to be resolved are the specifics that need be afforded in any particular case. It is generally conceded that a full trial, identical to that of a court of law, need not be provided. But the hearing provided must be more than an "informal review" and that the "rudiments of an adversary proceeding" should be preserved. Thus, it would seem that the student should be allowed to compel the use of witnesses, and where those involved are other students or faculty, this should present no problem. Important, however, as cross-examination may be in other contexts, it will no doubt be largely ineffectual for the high school student unless the more obvious need of some form of counsel is met. Thus, a high school senior was held to have the right to counsel in order to face a charge of cheating where the consequences would have been the denial of a state diploma and of certain scholarship and qualifying-exam privileges. But it has been held in another case that a mere "guidance conference" to determine whether a child suspended for misconduct may return to the school he had been attending or must be transferred to another does not require the presence of a lawyer. It appears, then, that there is a great deal of flexibility in procedural matters and that

19

a variety of factors, especially the seriousness of the penalty, will determine how far the courts will go in imposing procedural safeguards on school officials seeking to suspend or expel students.

There is an increasing trend of educational institutions reviewing their existing procedures to insure that they have adequate procedural machinery to implement the minimum standards already in force. More and more, disciplinary rules and regulations adopted by a school board dealing with student rights are set forth in writing and promulgated in handbooks and catalogues. The courts have urged the schools to provide that each disciplinary procedure incorporate some system of appeal.

It must be noted in any discussion of student rights that high school students, like others, are fully protected by the Fourteenth Amendment in their right to demonstrate. Furthermore, the courts have held that a rule requiring administrative approval before a public demonstration could take place on a college campus was an unconstitutional restraint on the students' First Amendment rights, requiring a reversal of their unlawful suspensions. Under proper conditions it appears that the same principle holds for high school campuses. However, where a student rally displays objectionable signs and broadcasts obscene expressions which threaten the maintenance of order on campus, or where students block access to school buildings, expulsions by the institution will be upheld. Similarly, a sit-in by students in campus buildings after hours may result in criminal convictions of trespass or unlawful assembly. Such results are consistent with providing a forum for all within narrow and reasonable restrictions that do no more than proscribe conduct unreasonable in terms of time, place, or manner.

The issue of religion in the schools has become of increasing importance in public education in recent years. The portion of the First Amendment with which we are concerned here provides that "Congress shall make no law respecting an establishment of religion, or prohibiting the free exercise thereof." While the First Amendment only prohibits Congress from making such laws, it is now established that this provision is made applicable to the states by the Fourteenth Amendment. It followes that neither Congress nor any state shall make any law respecting an establishment of religion or prohibiting the free exercise thereof. We are,

20

of course, concerned only with the principle as it relates to schools and their administration.

The legality of Bible reading and reciting prayers in the public school is an old problem. Until recent times about half the states permitted Bible readings in the schools, and in a few it was expressly prohibited. In a number of states such Bible reading was even required. At the present time, however, the Supreme Court of the United States has ruled such religious recitations as constituting a deprivation of the free exercise of religion or an establishment of religion within the meaning of the First Amendment. Students are not only not required to participate in such readings or prayers, but they must not even be witness to them in the classroom setting.

By the same token, the courts have been equally unequivocal about the observance of religious holidays on school premises. Symbols, songs, and other expressions of religious activities are strictly forbidden. In connection with Christmas festivities, however, some school districts have avoided legal actions through compromising programs in which the religions of all students are represented. However, the courts have been moving in the direction of respecting the rights of students who neither practice nor believe in any religion so that even the most innocuous activities are held to constitute an imposition of religious tenets upon nonbelievers. In short, the courts now refuse to permit even the slightest encroachment on the First Amendment.

Not only are school authorities forbidden to require students to participate in flag allegiance ceremonies when it is a violation of their established religious tenets (as in the case of Jehovah's Witnesses), but also to be excused from such participation. Students who choose to be excluded from these ceremonies must respect the right of those who do participate by in no way disrupting or obstructing the activity.

Generally speaking, rules and regulations of boards of education forbidding membership of pupils in secret organizations and providing punishment for violation of the rules by expulsion or declaring members ineligible to participate in certain school activities, have been upheld by the courts. The question is whether the rule regulating or forbidding membership in such organizations is reasonable. The cases upholding its reasonableness point out that secret societies have a marked influ-

21

ence on the school in that they tend to destroy good order, discipline, and scholarship. If this is true, the board has the authority to take appropriate action to prevent this influence. If the courts are of the opinion that such membership is not detrimental to the schools, a rule forbidding or regulating the organization will be held unreasonable and unenforceable.

The practice of pupils to marry before they are through school has become quite common. While this is particularly true of college and university students, the number of married pupils in high schools has increased substantially. What few cases there are involving the right of married pupils to attend school have resolved the question in favor of such right. As one court pointed out in ordering the admission of a married pupil, marriage is a domestic relation, highly favored by the law and that every child has a constitutional and statutory right to attend school, unless it can be proved that his moral conduct and standards are objectionable. Marriage itself is a highly approved moral act.

The rule is that school authorities are vested with sound discretion in the determination of whether a pupil has completed the requisite courses and possesses the necessary qualifications to entitle him to a diploma. But when it has been determined that the prescribed requisites have been met, the issuance of a diploma is a ministerial act which is mandatory. It has been held that a pupil may not be refused a diploma for refusal to wear a cap and gown at graduation exercises, although he may legally be denied the privilege of participation in the exercises. The discretion of the governing bodies of educational institutions will not be interfered with by the courts unless it appears that the refusal to issue a diploma is clearly unreasonable or arbitrary. For example, a student was denied a diploma because of his conduct between his final examinations, which he passed, and graduation. The court refused to interfere.

Chapter IV

YOUTH AND THE OWNERSHIP AND OPERATION
OF MOTOR VEHICLES

Purchase and Sale of Automobiles

An automobile is personal property which is different from
real property or real estate (land), and may be bought and sold,
or given away in the same manner as any other personal property.
As a minor, you are entitled to own personal property, but if
you sell it the person buying from you purchases at his own risk
since you are entitled to disaffirm the contract at any time after
that period. You should take the same precautions if you buy
an automobile from a minor and should refuse to buy unless his
parent or guardian gives written consent to the sale. Even then,
if the price is inadequate or unfair, you are taking a risk of having the sale set aside by a court acting at the request of the minor
party, the seller.

The purchase and sale of an automobile is a business transaction or contract, and any business transaction or contract of
a minor is subject to the supervision and regulation of the court
of the jurisdiction in which the minor lives or in which the transaction takes place. Until you become twenty-one your contracts,
sales or purchases may be set aside by the court if they are found
to be against your interests and if you acted without full knowledge and full protection.

If you attempt, as a minor to sell an automobile to a sec-
ond-hand dealer or to any other party, he probably will insist
upon having your parent's consent especially if the car appears
to be a good buy. In short, an adult who deals with a minor in
a commercial transaction does so at his own risk. The minor
who deals with an adult is a special ward of the court, entitled
to its protection. If you buy an automobile on time and are sued

for the balance of the purchase price the court may appoint a "special guardian" to protect your interests in the lawsuit, and to report to the court on the fairness of the transaction.

If you purchase an automobile before you attain your majority, and find that it is defective or even unsatisfactory, you may disaffirm the contract, return the automobile and get back your money. However, if you drive the car for a "reasonable time" after reaching your twenty-first birthday or whatever age in your state is designated as adulthood, you will be held to have affirmed the contract and will be denied relief. For example, you buy an automobile when you are nineteen and a half or even twenty years of age and offer to return it before you are twenty-one, the dealer will be required to refund all or a substantial part of your purchase price. But if you drive the car for any period of time after reaching your twenty-first birthday, the court may rule that you did not disaffirm your contract within a "reasonable time" and refuse to grant you relief. What constitutes a "reasonable time" will differ with each particular case, but it may be as long as three or four months and may be as short as one day. On the question of disaffirmance, the date on which you reached your majority becomes important and you should remember that it is not your birthday, but the day before your birthday on which you lose your right to disaffirm a disadvantageous or erroneous contract.

Registration of Motorized Vehicles

All motorized vehicles, whether motorcycles, automobiles, motorboats, or aircraft must be registered with the proper authorities. Motor vehicles are registered at your local motor vehicle bureau, one of which is located in county seats as well as in major cities of the state. Of course the main motor vehicle bureau office is situated in the capital of each state.

All motorized boats must be registered with the Treasury Department and some states and counties require registration of vessels operated on waters wholly within their boundaries. Local regulations differ, and if you intend to operate a power-propelled vehicle (even if it is a small rowboat with an outboard motor) you should be certain that in addition to your Federal registration you also comply with directives of the local authorities.

Aircraft must be registered with the Federal authorities and in addition many of the states require state registration. (For details of state registration requirements which apply equally to adults and minors, see Manual of Civil Aviation Law, published by Oceana Publications, Dobbs Ferry, N.Y.)

Operation and Insurance of Motorized Vehicles

In all states and territories a license is required to operate an automobile or other power-propelled vehicle operating on land. All states have a minimum age requirement, and in most states, a "learner's permit" is required before you are permitted to take a test. The usual procedure, upon attaining the age at which you may apply for a license is first to obtain a learner's permit and then, as soon as you feel that you are capable of passing the driving examination, to appear with a licensed driver to take your examination. A learner's permit does not give you the right to operate a motor vehicle unless a licensed operator is present with you in the vehicle.

In states which do not require a learner's permit, you should be extremely careful in operating a motor vehicle or taking instructions since you will be held strictly liable for any damage which you inflict on any person or property during the course of your instruction. Check at your state's local motor vehicle bureau to learn whether learner's permits are issued in your state.

Some states set a minimum age for operators and do not issue any type of license to any person below that age, while in other states a Junior License is issued. Table II lists the states in which a Junior License may be issued at age fourteen.

TABLE II

STATES IN WHICH A JUNIOR LICENSE MAY BE ISSUED AFTER YOU HAVE COMPLETED YOUR FOURTEENTH YEAR

Arkansas	Nevada
California	North Dakota

TABLE II (continued)

Florida	Ohio
Idaho	Oklahoma
Indiana	Oregon
Iowa	Tennessee
Kansas	Texas
Michigan	Wisconsin

Nebraska

In the states of New York, Pennsylvania and Vermont a Junior License may be obtained after you have completed your sixteenth year. In most states in which a Junior License is granted, however, it will not be granted to you as a matter of right, but some proof of the necessity for the license must be furnished to the local authorities. For instance, if you require the license to drive to school, or to assist your father at the farm, there will not be much difficulty in obtaining the license. If, however, you want the license merely to operate a "souped-up hot-rod" you may have difficulty in obtaining a Junior License in some jurisdictions. Most Junior Licenses are not unrestricted; in many cases the vehicle may be driven only when an adult is present or near and during daylight hours. The usual restriction is that a Junior License is valid for unaccompanied driving during the day, but is valid for night-time driving only when an adult is present in the car. In some states the accompanying adult is also required to be a licensed operator.

Table III lists the ages at which an ordinary operator's or chauffeur's license may be issued.

TABLE III

OPERATOR'S LICENSES ISSUED AT:

14 Years

New Mexico	South Carolina

26

TABLE III (continued)

15 Years

Illinois	Montana
Louisiana	South Dakota
Maine	Virginia
Minnesota	Wyoming
Mississippi	

16 Years

Alabama	Michigan
Arizona	Missouri
Arkansas	Nebraska
California	Nevada
Colorado	New Hampshire
Connecticut	North Carolina
Delaware	North Dakota
District of Columbia	Ohio
Florida	Oklahoma
Georgia	Oregon
Idaho	Rhode Island
Indiana (16 years and 1 month)	Tennessee
Iowa	Texas
Kansas	Utah
Kentucky	Washington
Maryland	West Virginia
Massachusetts	Wisconsin

17 Years
New Jersey

18 Years

New York	Vermont
Pennsylvania	

If you have held a Junior License, upon attaining the minimum age for an adult license, it is not necessary for you to take another test. Upon attaining the proper age you merely surrender your junior license and obtain the regular operator's or chauffeur's license. A chauffeur's license is necessary in most states if you are to drive commercially, that is for a living, and the usual difference is that a chauffeur's license must have your photograph attached to it while the ordinary operator's license merely requires a description, and your signature for purposes of identification.

Be particularly careful not to drive an automobile when you do not have a license. Not only is it a penal offense which may subject you to a fine or imprisonment or to treatment as a juvenile delinquent, but it may also invalidate insurance which your father or the other owner carries on the automobile. Most automobile liability insurance policies and many collision policies provide that the policy will not be effective and the owner of the vehicle will not be insured against liability or damage if the vehicle is operated by an unlicensed operator or by an operator under a certain minimum age. Since most states have financial responsibility laws, any judgment which may be recovered against you or your father will remain a lien against your property and earnings for twenty years and you will not be permitted to own or operate an automobile until the judgment is paid and satisfied in full. If you misstate your age, and obtain a license by telling the authorities that you are older than you actually are, the authorities may cancel your license and declare it void from the outset, thus putting you in the position of being an unlicensed operator, and invalidating your insurance.

In a great many states, insurance rates are increased if the household of the automobile owner contains one or more licensed drivers under certain minimum ages. These minimum ages vary from eighteen years in some states to twenty-six in others and any misstatement of a material fact, such as the age of the licensed operator, may be sufficient to void the policy. It is particularly important, therefore, to be completely honest, straightforward and above-board in your dealings with the public authorities and insurance companies.

In most states it is necessary to present a birth certificate to obtain both a learner's permit, a junior operator's license or an operator's or chauffeur's license. In some states you may obtain the permits or licenses by having one or more older persons vouch for you, but if you falsify or alter your birth certificate, or present false evidence as to your age this is a serious offense which may have a disastrous effect on your future. Time will go by rapidly enough and you should be particularly careful not to falsify any official records merely for the sake of driving a motor vehicle a few months earlier.

If you merely wish to operate your own small motorboat, you do not require a license. Some jurisdictions, however, having been plagued with "hot-rod speedboat operators" have enacted local statutes and ordinances setting minimum ages below which you may not be permitted to operate your motorboat. If you have any doubt of your eligibility, consult the local police in the town or village where you live.

However, in order to obtain a commercial license to operate a motorboat for hire, you must have attained the age of sixteen years and must obtain your license or papers from the United States Coast Guard which jurisdiction will have definite requirements for the particular type of license which you desire to obtain.

You may not operate any aircraft until you have attained the age of sixteen years. Unlike motorboats or motor vehicles you must be a citizen of the United States of America or of a foreign government which grants reciprocal student pilot privileges to citizens of the United States and you must read, write, and speak the English language. You do not need to know anything about aeronautics in order to obtain your student pilot certificate, but before you can make your first solo flight you must pass a written examination on certain of the Civil Air Regulations dealing with contact flight rules and must be found competent by a licensed instructor to make a solo flight, with such authority endorsed on your student pilot's certificate.

Although you may obtain a student pilot certificate at the age of 16 you may not receive your private pilot certificate until you have attained the age of seventeen years. Once you have obtained the certificate, however, it will remain in effect indefinitely unless it is suspended or revoked by the Civil Aeronautics Board.

In order to fly an aircraft for hire, you must pass further examinations and must have attained a minimum age of eighteen years while in order to be licensed as an airline transport pilot you must have attained the age of at least twenty-three years, be of good moral character, and be a high school graduate or have qualifications deemed by the Civil Aeronautics Administrator to be the equivalent of a high school education.

In order to obtain your private pilot's rating, you must have had fifteen hours of dual instruction by a rated flight instructor and twenty-five hours of solo practice, while in order to obtain your commercial pilot certificate, that is to fly an aircraft for hire, in addition to having completed your eighteenth year, you must have at least two hundred hours of credited flight time, including one hundred hours of flight as a pilot in command, of which five hours must have been flown within sixty days, and of which twenty-four must be of cross-country flight as pilot in command, including one flight of not less than three hundred fifty miles in the course of which three full-stop landings have been made at different points, and ten hours of night-flight time including not less than ten takeoffs and ten landings at night. The requirements for airline transport pilot are so rigorous that it is almost impossible to meet the qualifications of experience and flying time prior to completing your twenty-third year.

Chapter Five

YOUTH AND CONTRACTS INCLUDING
PERSONAL AND REAL PROPERTY

Contracts in General

A contract is a promise or set of promises, for repudiation or breach of which the law provides a remedy. It is, in effect, an agreement enforceable by law, giving rise to rights to receive some benefit, and duties or obligations to give or perform something of value, or to refrain from doing something. For example, if you sign a contract to buy an automobile, the dealer promises to deliver a car to you, and you promise to pay him. If you sign a contract to paint a house, your duty or obligation is to perform the work and your right, or benefit, is to be paid. If you sign a contract not to engage in a certain business in a specified area or location, your right is to receive money or other thing of value, and your duty is to refrain from engaging in the business.

Contracts consist of promises or understandings that something will happen, or will not happen in the future. Contracts may be expressed, when their terms are stated by the parties, or implied when their terms are not so stated, and are assumed or implied by operation of law. If you write an order for two tons of coal, agreeing to pay twenty-five dollars on delivery of the coal, you are party to an express contract, while if you go to the supermarket and take a package of food, or pick up a newspaper from the stand, there is an implied agreement or a contract on your part, to pay for the item taken.

Under American law, there are two ways in which promises may be made binding, and thereby may become contracts. The first is by giving the transaction a certain form, such as signing a formal written instrument or contract. The second is by mutual agreement, whether such agreement is express, as where

31

the parties have a specific understanding, or implied, where one party does an act which gives rise to an obligation on the part of some other party. When you sit down at the soda fountain and say "Two chocolate sundaes," you enter into an implied promise to pay for them at the going price, whatever that may be. On the other hand, if you ask "How much are these pencils you are selling?" and after being told that they are ten cents each, you put down a quarter and say "I'll buy two of them," there is an express contract, even though it is not in writing, since the storekeeper has made a specific offer to sell, and you have given him your unconditional acceptance.

The formation of a contract requires the existence of persons capable of entering into a contract. As an infant, there are few contracts into which you may enter. As a general rule, an infant's contract is voidable at the option of the infant, both during his infancy or minority and for a reasonable time after attaining his majority. If two adults make a contract pursuant to which Abner agrees to sell, and Benjamin agrees to buy Abner's 1954 Bearcat automobile for a thousand dollars, and Abner and Benjamin are both adults, both are bound. If Benjamin is an infant, however, he may, if he chooses, avoid the contract. If he states sometime after signing his name, that he does not want to go through with the deal, he is at perfect liberty to change his mind, and he is under no further obligation. If he is an adult, he will be required to pay damages to Abner for his repudiation or breach of contract.

As a minor, you lack the general capacity to make a contract, and your promises or agreements may be classified as void, voidable, or binding. There is no distinction made regarding your ability to enter into a contract if you are a minor of comparatively tender years, such as fourteen or fifteen, or whether you are twenty and, having nearly attained your majority, have ample intelligence in fact. Your written promise, as an infant, to be a surety on a bond, is void, and you cannot perform such an act, even with the consent of your guardian. On the other hand, your contract or written agreement to buy an automobile for a stated price is only voidable, and not void, and you may if you wish either insist on buying the automotile at the contract price, or cancel the contract, without any further obligation or expense to you.

In most states, you remain an infant until you attain your twenty-first year, although in some states (Arkansas, Idaho, Illinois, Maryland, Minnesota, Montana, Nevada, North Dakota, Oregon, South Dakota and Utah), if you are a female, you are granted contractual capacity (the ability to make a contract) when you attain your eighteenth birthday, or when you marry (in Alabama, California, Maryland, Nebraska, Oregon, Texas and Washington). In four states (Iowa, Kansas, Louisiana and Utah), if you are a male and marry, you acquire the power to make a contract despite your minority.

Contracts for Services or Employment

Despite a growing tendency to free minors from restrictions on their freedom to act during minority, in most states neither you nor your parents may be bound by any contract for your employment made without your parent's consent. While you owe your parents a duty of obedience, you may not be compelled to perform a contract of employment made for you by them. If you enter into a contract to perform certain acts for an employer, and you subsequently decide that for reasons sufficient to you, but not sufficient as a matter of law (such as having to miss seeing an interesting series of baseball games), you may break the contract and decline to work without being held liable for your prospective employer's damages, as would be the case if you were an adult, and broke your contract. A contract of employment, entered into while you are a minor, is voidable at your option or election. An exception to this rule is found when your contract of employment has been approved by a court. Minors engaged in the entertainment field usually present their proposed contracts of employment to a court for approval, and such contracts are approved only after close scrutiny to insure the protection of the minor, and the placing in trust for him or her of some appreciable part of the payments to be made, both before the contract is begun, and at any time during its performance.

Necessaries Supplied to an Infant

We have pointed out that your contracts as an infant may be classified as void, voidable or binding. As matters of public policy, the underlying basis of this rule is your protection as a minor as well as the protection of the public. As an infant, you may make yourself liable for goods or services necessary for your maintenance, health and welfare. What is necessary will be determined from your position in life. Even in the case of contracts for necessaries, however, you have privileges as an infant which cease upon your becoming an adult. If you order, receive and use ten dozen eggs at three dollars a dozen, when the current market price is seventy-five cents, as an adult you will be required to pay thirty dollars, the contract price, but as an infant you will be required to pay only seven dollars and fifty cents, the reasonable value of the necessaries which you purchased.

Once you have received and used or consumed necessaries, such as food, clothing or lodging, your infancy will not be a defense or a bar to the collection of the claim of the person or firm who supplied you with the items. The claim will be limited to the reasonable value of the items supplied, unless the reasonable value exceeds the contract price, in which event you will be required to pay only the contract price. On the other hand, even though your contract to purchase necessaries is in writing, you may cancel or avoid the contract at any time up to the actual delivery of the goods or performance of the services.

What goods or services are "necessaries" will depend upon your resources and your station in life. In line with the policy of protecting an infant whenever possible, the courts tend to limit the definition of necessaries as closely as possible. Normally necessaries are limited to food purchased for the infant or his family (that is, his wife and children, not his mother and father), clothing of a reasonable kind, and lodging. The Uniform Sales Act, which has been adopted as the law in most states of the United States defines necessaries as goods suitable to his actual requirements at the time of delivery. Under this rule, you will be liable for the reasonable value of a pair of everyday, ready-made shoes, but not for a pair of custon-made riding boots or sport shoes which are considered luxuries rather than necessaries.

The services of a physician or dentist as well as prescribed medicines or drugs are recognized as necessary, as are the funeral expenses for your husband or wife. An elementary education has always been regarded as necessary, and today we find a tendency to include the cost of education which will equip the infant to obtain and hold a position. Dancing lessons, flying lessons and such food items as confectionery, fancy fruit or pastry, liquors and tobacco are not necessaries, and if a merchant has been improvident enough to sell them to you on your own credit, he will have a difficult time collecting since the law will not impose a legal obligation on you to pay, despite your moral obligation to the seller. In all claims against you for education or tuition, anything beyond an elementary education will be closely scrutinized, and correspondence schools have not been permitted to recover from an infant the cost of his tuition or lessons supplied to him under a written agreement.

If you are a minor, and have a lawyer to protect your property rights, the lawyer ordinarily will not be permitted to enforce his claim for compensation, even after he has rendered the services, since you are not permitted to act without the intervention of your guardian. On the other hand, if you hire a lawyer to defend you against a criminal charge, whether it is a minor or major offense, or to get you out of fail, you will be responsible for the reasonable value of the lawyer's fees.

Disaffirmance of Contracts

Most contracts made by minors or infants (and you should keep in mind that the legal terms "minor" and "infant" are interchangeable) are avoidable at any time after you have attained your majority. If your contract is not one of those which is void, it remains valid until you take some act to avoid it. Any act which shows an intention not to stand on the contract usually is sufficient. Thus, an express letter to the other party to a contract that you choose to disaffirm, a tender to the seller of the goods received, or a demand for the delivery of goods transferred by you ordinarily will be sufficient to disaffirm the contract.

If you have received something of value, and you later want to disaffirm or rescind your contract, you cannot do so without giving the other party to the contract the right to recover from you the consideration which he delivered to you. This does not mean that when you disaffirm or cancel a contract, you must always tender to the other party the consideration (goods or money, etc.) which you have received, but usually you indicate your intention to disaffirm the entire transaction, leaving to both parties the burden or demanding and regaining whatever they have parted with. If you still have the property or money which you received in the transaction, you should offer to surrender it as a condition of your disaffirmance. If you have bought an automobile, and after driving it for a month, decide that you do not like it, the best way for you to disaffirm is to offer to return the auto, and at the same time to demand the return of your money. If you no longer have the car, you cannot hope for any measure of success in demanding the return of your money, and if the car, while in your possession, has depreciated, in most states you will not receive all of your money, but the original amount less a deduction for the depreciation or damage to the car while it was in your possession.

The trend in recent years has been toward limiting your right as an infant to disaffirm unless the notice of disaffirmance is coupled with a tender of the property or other consideration received by you. In a few states you may rescind or disaffirm without any conditions if you have not yet attained your eighteenth birthday, but must tender or offer to return what you have received if you want to disaffirm, after you have completed your eighteenth year. In view of the high level of general education which prevails today, the early sophistication of young people, and the tremendous volume of business which they transact on their own behalf, more and more states tend to require you to tender the entire consideration received by you when you take the step to disaffirm the contract.

In cases where you disaffirm or rescind the contract, you are allowed only one change of mind. Once you take a definite step to disaffirm, you cannot disaffirm your disaffirmance, and have a second change of heart and decide to stand on the contract.

As a word of caution, you should never disaffirm a contract unless you feel that you have been defrauded badly. While you may be entitled legally to change your mind, such conduct will be a black mark against you in the business world and will hurt your reputation for fair dealing among your acquaintances. It is far better to be known as one who took a small loss, or even a considerable loss, rather than as one who did not keep his bargain.

Contracts Which May Not Be Disaffirmed

For reasons of general public welfare, some contracts made

by infants cannot be disaffirmed. Contracts of enlistment in the Armed Forces have usually been made binding by statute, particularly where parental consent has been given prior to enlistment. Undertakings or promises to support your child or children or your wife, may not be avoided because of your minority. In some states voidable contracts become binding if the consideration which you receive has been used or dissipated, but in any event, it is best for you to consult a lawyer to learn your rights and obligations under the law of your particular jurisdiction. Bring some money with you, because the lawyer will know the law, and will realize that if he is not paid in advance, you may be able to disaffirm and avoid your obligation to him.

You should never, under any circumstances, enter into an agreement with the idea that if you do not like the bargain you can use your infancy as an excuse to crawl out or to avoid fulfilling your part of the bargain. Be particularly careful not to misrepresent your age, since such action constitutes fraud and deceit, for which you may be held liable as a tort or wrong, even if your obligations under the contract cannot be enforced against you because of your minority. In addition, if you are forced to bring suit through your general guardian or guardian ad litem, for a degree of judgment of a court of equity directing that your contract be cancelled or rescinded, you may learn to your disadvantage that the court will refuse to grant you relief because you do not come into court with clean hands, having yourself committed a wrong. In such an event, the court may decide to "leave you where it finds you," and may decline to grant you relief because of your own wrong.

Sales of Real Estate by a Minor

As an infant or minor, and remember that you will remain as such until you have attained your majority, you cannot by yourself convey a clear title to real estate. You can, however, pass a clear title if you apply to the court for the appointment of a guardian, and the court approved the sale through your guardian.

If you have inherited real estate from a relative or parent, and you feel that it is to your interest to sell the real estate, you should consult an attorney and permit him to make the application to the court for permission to sell. The court will then hear your attorney, and may sometimes call you for questioning, then appoint some unbiased person unconnected with the purchasers, to make a report on the adequacy of the price and the effect of the sale on you. If the court finds that the price is adequate, and that the sale will be to your best interests, a court order will be made approving the sale and sometimes fixing the amount of attorneys' fees to be paid. If the court does not approve the sale, you cannot convey a clear title and you will have difficulty in finding a seller to accept your conveyance and to pay you money for a conveyance.

Once in a great while you may find someone who is so anxious to buy the real estate that he is willing to take a chance and to hope that you will not disaffirm within a "reasonable time" after attaining the age of twenty-one years. If you have a chance to make a sale, you should consult your attorney and let him apply to the court.

Anyone who purchases real estate from you, however, even with the protection of a court order, does not have an absolute or clear title until the passage of a reasonable time after you have attained your twenty-first birthday. Of course, if you are ten, eleven or twelve years old you will not have very much to say about the transaction, and your guardian as well as the special guardian appointed by the court will make their reports and their advice will probably be accepted by the court. If, however, you have passed your sixteenth birthday and are between the ages of sixteen and twenty, the court will listen to you and ask you a number of questions to find out whether you want the sale and whether, if you want it, it is to your advantage.

Purchases by a Minor

You will encounter somewhat less difficulty in purchasing real estate, although any purchaser who conveys property to you will likewise run the risk of having you disaffirm the transaction and sue him for the return of your purchase price at any time prior to your attaining your majority or within a reasonable time after you attain your majority.

An owner of real estate who is particularly anxious to make a sale may even go so far as to offer to pay your lawyer's expenses and the court fees if you will apply to the court for permission to make the purchase. If, however, he is in a hurry and does not want to wait for the court proceedings, he may take the risk of your disaffirming your purchase and proceed with the closing of title.

He will do this, however, with the constructive knowledge that you may disaffirm, tender the property back to him and demand the return of the money which you have paid him.

If you are a minor and desire to become either a mortgagor or a mortgagee, you will encounter the same difficulty in mortgaging your own real property or in lending money. Any person lending you money on the security of your real estate may quite reasonably refuse to make the loan unless you obtain court permission. This will be based on court scrutiny of the agreement for the proposed mortgage and a determination that its terms are fair and reasonable.

If you acquire any considerable amount of money while you are still an infant and desire to lend it, the loan ordinarily will be subject to court approval, particularly if it is made by your guardian. However, if you have acquired money through your own efforts and not through inheritance, the money may be under your own control and not under that of a guardian, and in such circumstances there will be occasional transactions which may be made without the intervention of the court. However, if some relative or friend, or even if the court on its own motion ascertains that as a minor, you control considerable funds, you may find even against your wishes that a guardian will be appointed to assist you and to conserve your property for you until you reach your majority.

Minor as Landlord or Tenant

If you desire to rent or lease real property for your own use, you will have less difficulty in renting for residential purposes than for business purposes. If you rent an apartment or a house in which to live, your landlord ordinarily will not be too particular or too concerned about your minority if you can show him that you are of sufficient financial responsibility to pay the rent for the period of the lease. If you are close to your majority, that is within a year or eighteen months of attaining your majority, the landlord probably will not bother very much, but will accept your rent and permit you to occupy the premises, but if you are more than eighteen months away from your majority and the lease calls for the investment by the landlord of time, money and effort in improving the property for your occupancy, he may insist upon court approval before expending money to improve a leasehold, whereas a minor, you may repudiate it at any time before attaining your majority.

If you own real property and want to lease it to some other person for profit, the lessee, for his own protection, should ask for a court order approving the lease. If he does not do this he will merely have a month to month tenancy, terminable at your option, since as a minor or infant you may go into court at any time and ask that the lease or tenancy be set aside as contrary to your interests and as having been entered into without judicial approval.

As a general rule, you must have attained the age of twenty-one to serve as a real estate broker, and the age of eighteen to be licensed as a real estate salesman. Your own particular city, town, village or county, however, may have additional requirements, and before engaging in business, it is well to consult a local lawyer or real estate broker.

Inheritance

If your parents die without leaving a Will, you are entitled to receive a certain percentage of their estate. The percentage varies from state to state. In most cases, if one of your parents died intestate (without a Will), one-third will pass to your surviving parent, with the remaining two-thirds divided among you and your brothers and sisters. If one of your brothers and sisters has died before your parent, the share of the deceased brother or sister will be divided equally among you and your surviving brothers and sisters unless the deceased brother or sister left surviving children, in which event his or her share will be divided equally among such surviving children.

If you have not yet attained your majority at the time of the distribution of the estate, the property will be placed in the hands of your guardian. Ordinarily your surviving parent will serve as your guardian unless the deceased parent appointed some other person to hold your property for you. The guardian ordinarily will be required to file a bond and will be ordered to account from time to time to the Probate, Surrogate or Orphans Court, reporting the amount of principal and income received and the amount disbursed for your maintenance, welfare and education. As guardian, he usually receives a commission which ranges from one to five percent of the value of the property or funds which he handles. You are not permitted to receive either real property or personal property in your own name until you have attained your majority. While you are a minor, your property is subject to administration by your guardian under the supervision of the Court. If you feel that your guardian is not administering your estate properly, you may complain to the Court, and may compel him to account. If the Court finds that he has spent money improvidently or has made investments indicating an abuse of discretion, he may be required to repay to your estate any damages caused by his lack of judgment or indiscretion.

When your guardian files his report, whether it is an annual, semi-annual or biennial report, the Judge of the Court in which he files it may examine it himself or, in large cities such as New York, Chicago or Los Angeles, he may appoint a "Special Guardian" to read the report or inventory and then make a report to the Court advising the Court whether, in his opinion, the account is proper. The Special Guardian will make recommendations which, as a rule, will be followed by the Court. The Special Guardian is usually a lawyer, and the Court fixes his fee, which is then paid out of your property if the account is proper, or by your guardian if the account is improper.

Once you attain your majority your guardian will be discharged and you will be permitted to control your property yourself unless your parent or other benefactor has provided that your property remain in trust for a longer period of time. The usual provision is to provide that the principal be held in trust but that the income be paid to you from time to time, which will be in quarterly installments, to permit you to attend school and to maintain yourself until you attain your majority.

Except in the state of Louisiana your parents are not required to leave you anything by Will, and they may disinherit you. In Louisiana they must leave you some part of their estate. In all other jurisdictions they may cut you off entirely, although unless they mention you in the Will, merely by stating that they have made adequate provision or that for reasons sufficient to them they do not leave anything to you, you may contest the Will. If you feel that you have been treated unfairly or that someone has unduly influenced one of your parents you should consult an attorney and permit him to examine the facts of the case.

Execution of a Last Will and Testament

If you die without a Last Will and Testament the law will, in effect, make a Will for you and will provide for the distribution of your property. If you are under twenty-one and die without a will, your property ordinarily will pass to your parents. If your parents are not living it usually will pass to your brothers and sisters. Of course, if you are married and have children, the entire estate will pass to your wife and children, and if you are married and have no children, a certain amount will pass to your wife or husband and the balance to your other relatives, with your mother and father taking before your brothers and sisters.

Once you have attained the minimum age, however, you are permitted to execute a Last Will and Testament. In most states the minimum age for the execution of a Will is twenty-one years. The age varies from state to state, however, and in Georgia and Puerto Rico it is as low as fourteen, while in South Carolina, a girl twelve years of age may make a Will of personal property. In all such instances, however, a more advanced age is required for the disposition of real property. Table IV sets forth the ages at which you may make a Last Will and Testament of real and personal property. In most states your marriage before you reach the minimum age does not constitute an emancipation or enable you to make a Will. However, in Arizona, New Hampshire, Washington and Wisconsin, your marriage will emancipate you and will permit you to execute a valid Will.

TABLE IV

MINIMUM AGE REQUIREMENT FOR
THE EXECUTION OF A WILL

STATE	Minimum Age of will for Real Property	Minimum Age of will for Personal Property
Alabama	21	18
Alaska	21	21
Arizona	21 or married	21 or married
Arkansas	21	18
California	18	18
Colorado	18	18
Connecticut	18	18
Delaware	18	18
Dist. of Columbia	Male--21 Female--18	Male--21 Female--18
Florida	18	18
Georgia	14	14
Hawaii	20	20
Idaho	18	18
Illinois	18	18
Indiana	21	21
Iowa	21	21
Kansas	21	21
Kentucky	21	21
Louisiana	16	16
Maine	21 or married woman or widow	21 or married woman or widow
Massachusetts	21	21
Michigan	21	21
Maryland	Male--21 Female--18	Male--21 Female--18
Minnesota	21	21
Mississippi	21	21
Missouri	Male--21 Female--21	Male--18 Female--21
Montana	18	18

43

TABLE IV (continued)

STATE	Minimum Age for will of Real Property	Minimum Age for will of Personal Property
Nebraska	21	21
Nevada	18	18
New Hampshire	18 or married	18 or married
New Jersey	21	21
New Mexico	21	21
New York	21	18
North Carolina	18	18
North Dakota	18	18
Ohio	21	21
Oklahoma	18	18
Oregon	21	21
Pennsylvania	21	21
Philippines	18	18
Puerto Rico	14	14
Rhode Island	21	18
South Carolina	21	21
South Dakota	18	18
Tennessee	18	18
Texas	21 or married	21 or married
Utah	18	18
Vermont	21	21
Virginia	21	18
Washington	21 or 18 if married or in Military Service	
West Virginia	21	21
Wisconsin	21 or married woman, 18 or over, or any minor in Military Service	
Wyoming	21	21

If you have determined from the Table that you are old enough to make a Will, you should confer with a lawyer.

Before consulting your lawyer, however, (AND YOU SHOULD NOT ATTEMPT TO DRAW A WILL WITHOUT CONSULTING A LAWYER), it may be advisable for you to read "The Law of Wills," Vol. 2, Legal Almanac Series.

Chapter Six

YOUTH AND RIGHTS AND OBLIGATIONS
ARISING FROM TORTS

Different Types of Torts

A tort is a wrong or violation of your personal or property rights. Ordinarily it is accompanied by a right to recover damages from the person responsible. Your minority has an effect both on your tort rights and on your tort liabilities. If you are injured, you and your parents have a right to recover from the person responsible for the wrong, whether the wrong was unintentional or negligent, or whether it was inflicted willfully and deliberately. An example of an unintentional wrong is your being struck by an automobile, while a willful and deliberate tort would be an unprovoked assault by someone with a real or fancied grievance against you.

Even a real grievance does not give a person the right to inflict physical punishment or harm, and you will have a right to recover. In some cases where the tort or wrong is intentional and deliberate, you will be entitled to recover additional or punitive damages. Damages which will be awarded for tort liability may be of a great variety, both as to type and amount. There may be actual damages for property destroyed (the replacement value less depreciation), direct or special damages such as the payment of medical bills and lost earnings, damages for pain and suffering which cannot be measured by any fixed yardstick, damages for permanent disability, disfigurement or discomfort which likewise are a matter of speculation, and punitive damages which are imposed both by way of compensation and by way of punishment or deterrent from further or similar wrongdoing.

Rights to Recover Damages for Torts Inflicted Upon an Infant

When you are injured during your minority, rights of action arise immediately in your favor and in favor of your father (or your mother if your father is deceased), for the amount necessarily expended or to be expended for your care and treatment, convalescence and lost earnings.

You may bring an action and recover not only against the person directly responsible for your injury (such as the driver of an automobile) but also against any person who may have contributed in any way to your injury (such as the owner of the automobile who permitted the driver to use it). Likewise, if you are injured in a building you may recover against the landlord if he had actual notice of a defective condition and failed to repair it, and against the tenant if it was also the tenant's responsibility to repair the premises and keep them safe for persons lawfully entering them.

You are always entitled to recover for your pain and suffering. The amount varies both from case to case, and from state to state. In the more populous states, verdicts and settlements usually are larger than in the less densely inhabited areas. Recovery for pain and suffering vary and will, in a large measure, be determined by your doctor's reports. It is particularly important therefore, when you are injured, to see that you are provided with immediate and constant medical advice and supervision, necessary not only for your recovery and physical well-being, but also for your ability to recoup your losses from the person or persons responsible for your injury. Both the person responsible, his lawyer and his insurance carrier will rely heavily on the doctor's report, even though they will ask, with perfect propriety, that you be examined by their doctor. If their own doctor's report coincides with the report of the doctor who has cared for you, you have made a substantial step towards the settlement of your claim even if there is some question of liability or responsibility for the wrong.

Ordinarily, if you are a minor, your father is responsible for your medical care and treatment, and for your doctor bills, and in addition to your own action for pain and suffering, disfigurement or permanent disability, your father will have a cause of action to recover for past and prospective medical expenses.

For example, if you receive an injury which will require massage for a period of years, the court may not only award your father an amount for monies spent to date but may include damages for a period of one, two, three or even five years for future treatment or rehabilitation. The same applies if successive operations will be necessary to restore you to the physical condition of health which you enjoyed prior to the accident.

Theoretically, until you attain your majority your earnings belong to your father, but if you can show a course of conduct whereby your own earnings had been placed in the bank, you yourself may be entitled to recover for them. In most states you will be entitled to recover for the period of your disability even if your employer was kind enough to pay you for that period, or if you had an insurance policy which covered lost earnings. In a few states however, you may recover or recoup only for what you actually lost and if your employer paid your salary or if you had an insurance policy covering wages lost during the time of your injury or disability, you will not be permitted to recover from the person inflicting the wrong.

In many states these are causes of action which exist in your favor as an infant, which would not exist had you attained your majority. For instance, if you enter places of amusement and take part in hazardous amusement, as an adult, you are held to have assumed the risk of injury, but as an infant, in many jurisdictions, you are not permitted to waive your rights to recover for injury and are not considered legally capable of assuming a risk. In many other instances an adult must prove that the person inflicting the injury did a wrongful act or committed an intentional tort but an infant, merely by being placed in the position of injury and by being an infant, may recover.

Right of an Infant to recover for Injury or Death of Parent or Guardian

If your father, as the breadwinner of your family, is killed in an accident, the entire family has the right to recover damages from the person or corporation responsible for his death. These damages may include not only his medical bills and funeral bills but also damages for his pain and suffering until the time of his death and for his prospective lost earnings. The prospective lost earnings will be apportioned among the surviving widow and surviving children, in accordance with their life expectancy and expectancy of support from the father.

If your mother is thirty-eight years of age and you are eighteen and have three brothers and sisters age sixteen, fourteen and eleven respectively, your mother will be entitled in the normal course of events to support from your father for his life expectancy or her life expectancy, whichever may be shorter.

Let us assume that at the time he was killed in an accident, your father was forty-four years of age and your mother thirty-eight years of age. Although your mother has life expectancy of twenty-nine years, she will be entitled to support only for your father's expectancy which at that particular age was twenty-five years. You will be entitled to support for three more years, your sixteen-year-old brother for five more years, your fourteen-year-old brother for seven more years and your eleven-year-old sister for ten more years.

Let us assume that your father earned five thousand dollars a year and that there was absolute liability. The loss of earnings amounting to one hundred twenty-five thousand dollars (in theory since the jury or Court establishing the damages may take other factors into consideration) will be divided by giving one-half to your mother and by apportioning the remaining one-half or sixty-two thousand five hundred dollars among you and your brothers and sister in accordance with your own particular age and expectancy of support. You will receive three twenty-fifths or $7,500, your sixteen-year-old brother will receive five twenty-fifths or $12,500, your fourteen-year-old brother will receive seven twenty-fifths or $17,500, while your eleven-year-old sister will receive ten twenty-fifths or $25,000.

Any settlement where your rights as infants are involved will be subject to the approval of the court which will also fix the attorney's fee, and which will not permit you to pay your attorney a fee in excess of one-third of the amount recovered, and will not permit you to accept an inadequate settlement.

Liability for Torts Committed by Infants

You yourself, even though an infant, may be held liable for **any tort** or wrong which you commit or inflict upon another. If you do not have any property you cannot, of course, be made to pay any judgment against you, but the judgment will remain a lien for twenty years and may be enforced against your earnings or any property which you acquire as you grow older. In addition, your parents may be subjected to liability in certain specifically enumerated instances.

As a rule, a parent or guardian is not responsible for the torts of a child but there are three specific exemptions. If the parent or guardian actually directs or orders the child to commit it when he could stop him, the parent will be hend liable. If you and your father walk down the street past a greenhouse and your father, wanting to test the strength of your arm, suggests to you that you throw bricks through the greenhouse windows, he as well as you will be liable for the tort. In such circumstances, you as an infant might even be excused since you would be held merely to have obeyed your parent and to have been incapable of forming the necessary specific intent required to subject you to liability. Even if your father made a passive suggestion such as "Those windows look very inviting for flying stones" he could be held responsible for your action if a judge or jury found as a matter of fact that in making the remark your father was in effect making a suggestion to you.

The second exception to the rule which imposes on your parent the responsibility for a wrong committed by you during your minority is the case where your parent knows that you have a dangerous or vicious propensity, or habits or patterns of behavior which result in damage. In this exception are cases where your parent furnishes you with the instrument which does the damage such as an air rifle, .22 caliber rifle, or even a football or baseball which is driven through a plate-glass window. If your parent could have anticipated as a reasonable man, that the toy or object which he gave you might result in damage he will be held liable to anyone suffering damage even though he was not present at the time the wrong was committed by you, and even though the toy itself was comparatively innocent.

The third exception is the "family car." In almost all states the owner of a motor vehicle will be responsible for any damage done by any person operating the vehicle with his permission. Even in those states which do not have this rule of strict liability imposed upon the owner of a car, or head of a family where damage is done by his automobile when it is operated by any member of the family. You should keep this in mind when your father occasionally tells you that you may not use the family car, and you should also remember that if you take the car, you will be presumed to have operated it with his permission and that your negligence may result in a judgment against your father which may take away from the entire family the home in which you live.

Chapter Seven

YOUTH, DRUGS AND ALCOHOL

Drugs

Possessing, distributing, selling, or manufacturing certain drugs in the United States is a serious crime because it affects the health and well-being of people. An authoritative definition of drug addiction, widely accepted, is that promulgated by the World Health Organization:

"Drug addiction is a state of periodic or chronic intoxication, detrimental to the individual and to society, produced by the repeated consumption of a drug (natural or synthetic). Its characteristics include: (1) an overpowering desire or need (compulsion) to continue taking the drug and to obtain it by any means; (2) a tendency to increase the dose; (3) a psychic (psychological) and sometimes a physical dependence on the effects of the drug."

Drugs are two-edged swords--they may save lives or wreck lives. Historically men have used and misused drugs since ancient times. In our society an increasing variety of dangerous and harmful drugs is being misused by an increasing number of people-- including the young. The most commonly used drugs can be divided into four categories: (1) hallucinogens: marijuana and hashish, LSD, DMT, mescaline, etc.; (2) depressants: barbiturates (Seconal, Nembutal); tranquilizers (Miltown, Equanil); (3) stimulants: amphetamines (Benzedrine, Dexedrine, Methedrine, Ritalin); diet pills (Preludin); (4) narcotics: heroin, codeine, morphine, Demerol.

51

Penalties for Drug Abuse and Violations

Penalties are severe for use and possession of narcotic drugs and marijuana. While there is much debate as to whether the same penalties should apply to the use and possession of marijuana as to "hard drugs" like heroin, regardless of one's belief in the wisdom and justice of the drug laws, it is important to comply with them until they are changed. A conviction for a crime, no matter whether or not the law which was violated is repealed later, stays on one's record for life and can seriously jeopardize one's career as pointed out in our chapter on criminal law.

Under Federal Law possession of narcotic drugs (marijuana is in this category) is a felony. Federal laws covering depressant, stimulant, and hallucinogenic drugs (like LSD) involve penalties of from one to six years' imprisonment, and fines up to $15,000, depending upon the offense. Steps are being taken by the federal government to help drug users between the ages of 18 and 23. Under the Youth Rehabilitation Act, the drug user is sent to a rehabilitation center for 18 months, followed by a six-month probation period. If after two years the person remains a law-abiding citizen, the record is expunged.

All states except California have adopted the Uniform Narcotics Drug Act. While all of the states enacting this legislation which is aimed at protecting those using narcotics legally and penalizing those using such drugs illegally, each of them have various minor provisions dealing with terminology.

The provisions of the Penal Law of New York State will be sketched here as an example of the kind of laws which prevail in this country dealing with drug abuse.

It is a violation to appear in a public place under the influence of a dangerous drug.

Mere possession of a dangerous drug is a misdemeanor. One germinating seed of marijuana is all that is necessary for possible conviction.

It is a misdemeanor to loiter or remain in any place with one or more persons for the purpose of unlawfully using or possessing a dangerous drug; for example, attending and participating in "pot" parties.

It is a misdemeanor for anyone to possess or sell a hypodermic needle or any other instrument which could be used for the administering of any narcotic drug without a doctor's prescription.

It is a crime to operate a motor vehicle under the influence of a dangerous drug. The first offense, if convicted, is a misdemeanor. A second offense within ten years is a felony.

The presence of a dangerous drug in an automobile makes the automobile subject to seizure and impounding until application for the return of the vehicle is made to the appropriate court. Whether or not the drugs are in open view, all persons in the vehicle are presumed to have possession in the eyes of the law. Depending on the amount of the drugs, the charge can be a misdemeanor or a felony.

Anyone who possesses a dangerous drug with intent to sell (including giving away, bartering, or dispensing) is committing a felony and he is subject to a penalty of up to four years in a state prison. If the sale is to a minor, the possible sentence can be up to 25 years. This includes the youngster who gives away one marijuana cigarette to another minor.

Anyone possessing heroin, morphine, cocaine, or opium in quantity of eight ounces or more commits a felony punishable by up to 25 years in prison. If the quantity is one pound or more, the individual is guilty of a felony which may be punishable by up to life in prison.

Under New York State law, it is possible to sentence a narcotics addict (not indlucing marijuana) to 18 months at a rehabilitation center to be followed by 18 months of probation. If the probation is violated, the narcotics user is sent back to a maximum security rehabilitation center for another 18 months. If there is a third violation of probation, the judge may sentence the user under the original criminal charge.

Juveniles (over 7 and under 16 years) who are arrested on drug charges are generally referred to local family courts and charged with juvenile delinquency. After a hearing, the Family Court judge decides on the type of treatment and/or detention that he considers best for the offender. The names of juveniles under arrest are not released to the public.

Alcohol

Each state determines the age at which young people are allowed to buy and consume alcoholic drinks. It is illegal for young people to buy or accept drinks before that age. An adult who buys alcohol for or gives such a drink to a minor is also committing an illegal act.

In most states the law does not prohibit you from taking a drink, but in some states the person who gives you the drink or furnished it to you is guilty of a crime or misdemeanor. In many places there will be no crime or misdemeanor unless you become ill or intoxicated and in that event the person who gave you the drink will be held to have contributed to the delinquency of a minor. In some states you are permitted to make purchases of intoxicating beverages if you can furnish the seller with the written consent of your parent. Most dispensers of intoxicating beverages, however, are unwilling to risk arrest or revocation of their licenses by selling to minors even with written consent.

All states have alcoholic beverage control laws and one of the most serious offenses which may be charged against a licensee is that he sold to minors. In addition to suspension and revocation of license, criminal penalties are provided in every state. A growing number of states penalize minors for misrepresenting their ages but the responsibility still rests upon the seller to insist upon proof of age before making a sale. Some states require a birth certificate to prove that you have reached your twenty-first birthday before you can be served intoxicating beverages. In other states registration cards are issued and if shown to the seller, are a defense to any licensee charged with selling liquor to minors. But in a majority of states knowledge of the seller is immaterial and the offense is committed when a sale is made to a minor regardless of the good faith of the seller or reasonable error in judging age. If you appear to be younger than your actual age it is wise to carry with you your birth certificate, automobile license, or draft registration card as proof of your age.

Chapter Eight

YOUTH AND THE CRIMINAL LAW

Juvenile Delinquency

In all states, until you have reached your fifteenth birthday, you may not be convicted of any crime except a willful premeditated murder (murder in the first degree) or a murder committed in anger, but with the intent to take a human life (murder in the second degree). Other offenses will be acts of juvenile delinquency, even if they are so serious as to be classified as felonies.

Once you have attained your sixteenth birthday, however, the picture changes and you may then be convicted of a felony, misdemeanor or an offense such as disorderly conduct. In most states, until you have attained your sixteenth birthday you will be treated as a juvenile delinquent if your offense is anything less than murder. Thereafter, you may be treated either as a juvenile delinquent, a "youthful offender" or in the same manner as any adult charged with a similar offense. As a general rule you may expect leniency until you have reached your sixteenth birthday and thereafter you may expect to be treated as an ordinary offender or criminal, particularly if you have a previous record. The age limit for juvenile courts in cases of delinquent boys is sixteen in five states, and eighteen years or higher in thirty-one states. In some states the Juvenile Court has discretion to accept, on transfer from the ordinary Criminal Courts, minors above the age limit for exclusive original jurisdiction. Table V sets forth the limits of the ages at which you will be treated as a juvenile delinquent. Once you have attained the age set forth you may no longer be treated as a juvenile delinquent but will be treated as an ordinary criminal, or at best as a "youthful offender."

TABLE V

AGES AT WHICH YOU CEASE TO BE TREATED
AS A JUVENILE DELINQUENT

Alabama	18
Alaska	18
Arizona	18
Arkansas	21
California	21
Colorado	16--if offense punishable by death or life imprisonment, otherwise 18
Connecticut	16
Delaware	18
Dist. of Columbia	18
Florida	18
Georgia	16
Hawaii	18
Idaho	18
Illinois	Boys--17, Girls--18
Indiana	18--except where punishable by death or life imprisonment, then 16
Iowa	18
Kansas	16
Kentucky	Boys--17, Girls--18 even in murder cases
Louisiana	17 with optional jurisdiction to 21
Maine	17
Maryland	varies from 16 to 18 in different counties
Massachusetts	17
Michigan	17 with concurrent jurisdiction over children 17 to 19
Minnesota	18
Mississippi	18
Missouri	17
Montana	18
Nebraska	18
Nevada	18
New Hampshire	18
New Jersey	varies from 16 to 18

TABLE V (continued)

New Mexico	18
New York	16
North Carolina	16 (certain felonies punishable by 10 years imprisonment)
North Dakota	18
Ohio	18
Oklahoma	18
Oregon	18
Pennsylvania	18
Rhode Island	18 but jurisdiction may be waived
South Carolina	16 to 18
South Dakota	18
Tennessee	varies from 16 to 18, generally 17
Texas	Boys--17, Girls--18
Utah	18
Vermont	16
Virginia	varies from 18 to 21
Washington	18
West Virginia	18
Wisconsin	18 but offenders over 16 may be transferred to Criminal Courts
Wyoming	Boys--19, Girls--21

If you commit a federal offense and are under the age of eighteen, your case will be transferred to a State Juvenile Court in the State of your residence, or if you consent and the United States Attorney General has not expressly directed a contrary procedure, you may be proceeded against as a juvenile delinquent in the United States District Court.

Offenses

Legally speaking, an "offense" is a violation of law not sufficiently serious to be punished by confinement for more than a month. It is a violation of law for which you may not be indicted, and which usually is triable summarily before a Judge without a jury, and punishable by a fine rather than imprisonment or confinement. Ordinary traffic violations or smoking in the subway are examples of offenses. "Offenses" may be disposed of by the Court calling in your parents, and suggesting the imposition of family discipline, by placing you on probation, or by the more serious step of treating you as a wayward minor or a juvenile delinquent. This drastic proceeding, however, is usually followed only where you show signs of becoming unruly or anti-social, or of becoming involved in more serious difficulties with the law if you are not guided by a firm restraining hand.

Misdemeanor

A misdemeanor is a breach of the criminal law, more serious than an offense but not as serious as a felony. Ordinarily the punishment for a misdemeanor does not exceed a fine of one thousand dollars or confinement to jail for one year, but penalties vary in different states. If you have not yet attained the age set forth in Table V you may not be convicted of a misdemeanor, and the violation of law which, if you were an adult would be considered a misdemeanor becomes an act of juvenile delinquency. You should realize, however, that as a minor who has passed the age at which you cease to be treated as a juvenile delinquent you may be convicted of a misdemeanor and be subject to a sentence commeasurate with your offense, and to having a criminal record.

Felonies

A felony is a serious crime usually punishable by death or imprisonment in a state penitentiary. If you have not yet attained the age at which you will no longer be treated as a juvenile delinquent, you may not be charged with any felony other than murder and any other violation of law will be dealt with under the laws applicable to juvenile delinquency. Therefore, as a minor, you may not be charged with a "felony murder." A "felony murder" is a homicide committed in the course of any felony such as robbery, arson, burglary, larceny or rape. Adult offenders who undertake the commission of such felony, and, in the course of such felony bring about the death of a human being, are held to have committed a "felony murder," and if found by the jury to have perpetrated the acts, are guilty of murder in the first degree.

58

As a minor, you cannot be guilty of a felony and therefore you cannot be guilty of a "felony murder."

Wayward Minors

If you have passed the age at which you have ceased to be treated as a juvenile delinquent but have not yet attained your majority, and you develop bad habits or associate with bad companions to such an extent that you become a problem to your family and in society, you may be adjudged a wayward minor and placed on parole or probation for a period not to exceed two years. This period of parole or probation may not ordinarily include the last year of your minority, and if by reason of previous delinquency or for any other reason satisfying the Juvenile Court, you are not considered to be a fit subject for probation, you may be committed to any religious, charitable or reformative institution authorized by law to receive commitments of persons over the age of sixteen years. Your commitment, irrespective of your age at the time of commitment will be for an indeterminate period not to exceed three years. If you are committed to a religious institution, the institution as far as practicable will be one governed by persons of your own religious faith.

In determining whether you are a wayward minor, attitudes, acts and offenses in addition to violations of law are considered. The Juvenile Court before whom you appear may also adjudge you a wayward minor if you have been willfully disobedient to the reasonable and lawful commands of your parents, guardian or other custodian.

You may also be adjudged a wayward minor if you use drugs or intoxicating liquors to excess (and this is a rather elastic word), if you habitually associate with dissolute persons or persons with criminal records or bad reputations, or if you are found in places of ill repute. As a general rule, if you are a minor it is well to stay away from places of dubious reputation including specifically those classified by the Armed Forces as "Off Limits."

If you have passed the age where you may no longer be dealt with as a juvenile delinquent, but have not yet attained your majority, any misdemeanor or felony will subject you to having a "criminal record" which may not be removed from your name without an executive pardon by the Governor or President. This means that if you are charged with, and found guilty of a misdemeanor or felony, even one of the "minor felonies," you will have a criminal record for as long as you live. You may find yourself barred from civil service positions, from advancement or even enlistment in the armed forces, and from positions of trust in private business. For instance, you may have had a conviction for larceny, or automobile theft, when you were eighteen years of age. You may find it difficult to obtain a position in a bank, or with an insurance company, or even in a commercial organization where you would be required to handle funds.

Recognizing that young men and women sometimes become involved in serious difficulties without realizing the importance to their future and without having sufficient maturity to form a guilty intent, many states have established by statute a "youthful offender" proceeding. If you have passed the age in which you may be treated as a juvenile delinquent, but have not yet reached the age of nineteen years (this varies and in some states it is as high as twenty-one and in some as low as seventeen), you may, if found suitable after study by the court or its probation staff, or by the District Attorney, apply to the court to be treated as a "youthful offender."

If you are charged with a crime or a misdemeanor which is not punishable by death or life imprisonment, and if you have not previously been convicted of a felony, you may be sufficiently fortunate to be treated as a "youthful offender" instead of as an adult offender.

Where a grand jury has found an indictment for a felony, or where you have been charged by information (not by action of the grand jury, but by action of the District Attorney) with the commission of a misdemeanor, the District Attorney or prosecuting officer may make a recommendation to the Court, or your own lawyer, family, social worker or clergyman may ask the Court to make an investigation. Sometimes the Court on its own motion an investigation to determine whether you are eligible for treatment as a youthful offender. If your past record and possibility of future usefulness to society, to your family and to yourself merits such treatment, the indictment or information will be sealed and will not be opened to the general public.

If you have previously been convicted of a felony, you will not be eligible for treatment as a youthful offender, and if you have a bad record for violence and troublemaking and are involved in a robbery or in some offense involving assault against a person the chances of you being sufficiently fortunate to obtain youthful offender treatment are not favorable. On the other hand, if you have a good record, have been an obedient and dutiful son or daughter, with a school record that is average or better, and are involved in the only "scrape" of your life, your chances of obtaining the leniency incidental to youthful offender treatment are excellent.

If you enter a plea of "not guilty" or "guilty," the court may hold a trial to determine whether you may be adjudged a youthful offender. At that trial the persons who are the victims of the crime, the arresting officer, your teachers, clergymen, parents, neighbors and friends may be called upon to testify to permit the judge to decide, without the assistance of a jury, whether you may be treated as a youthful offender. If you are adjudged a "youthful offender" the indictment or information which has previously been filed against you will be considered a nullity and of no force and effect. You will thereupon be placed at the disposal of the Court which may commit you to confinement for a period not to exceed three years. The commitment may be either to any reformative institution or to a religious or charitable institution. As in the case of a wayward minor, you are to be committed wherever practicable to a religious institution of your own faith. The Court may then decide not to commit you at all and may either suspend sentence, if your record has been good up to the time of the offense, or impose sentence and suspend the execution of the sentence, placing you on probation for a period up to three years. This probation may be extended at any time before its expiration to a period not to exceed five years. Probation may be strict, requiring you to report once a week or even more often, or may be rather lenient permitting you to report on one occasion each month or two.

If you are found to be a youthful offender, this conviction will not operate to disqualify you from holding any public office, employment, civil service position or license granted by the public authorities, and you will not be considered a criminal nor will the determination be considered a conviction. Your fingerprints photographs and physical description will not become public records, but will be considered confidential.

In determining whether you are a youthful offender or may be treated as a youthful offender, your age at the time of the commission of the offense rather than your age at the time of the hearing will determine whether or not you are not entitled to the benefits of youthful offender procedure.

Chapter Nine

YOUTH AND THE OBLIGATIONS OF SUPPORT
AND TO BE SUPPORTED

In almost all states there are criminal statutes in force
making it a penal offense for a father to neglect to support his
children. These laws apply to fathers above and below the age
of twenty-one.

Rights of Minors to Support

As a minor unable to support yourself, or unable to support
yourself adequately, you are entitled to support from your parents
or from relatives standing in the place of parents. The primary
obligation to support minor children rests upon your father, and
if your father does not support you voluntarily, you or someone
acting in your behalf may apply to Court and compel him to support you in accordance with his means and earning ability. The
amount of support which he will be required to furnish will vary
not only from state to state, but also from community to community within the state, and according to his earning ability, income and property, and your own particular requirements.

If your father earns only $100 a week, and you do not require
any extraordinary medical care, a Court may direct him to pay
as little as $10 a week. On the other hand, if your father earns
$100,000 a year, the Court may direct him to pay your expenses
at preparatory school or college, and may order him to pay for
your benefit as much as one hundred dollars a week over the entire year. If you need extraordinary medical or surgical care
your father may be required to pay even more. If your father
had a high-salaried position from which he resigned, not for reasons of health, but because he did not want to work, the Court
may fix his obligation in accordance with what it thinks he could

earn if he exercised his earning ability honestly. If he does not work, he may be assessed a comparatively large amount if he has property which can be applied to your support, and he may even be ordered to pay out of capital an amount in excess of his income.

In determining the amount of support, the Court will also take into consideration the other obligations of your father, including the other persons for whose support he is liable. If he has not been paying the full amount of your support, and one of his other dependents becomes of age, you may reasonably expect the Court to order an increase.

If your father is deceased, or if he cannot be found, or is unable to support you, you may look to your mother, if she has the means to support you, or to your grandparents, on both your father's side or your mother's side of the family.

If support is furnished either by the State or by some person other than your parents, the persons furnishing support or the State itself has a right to sue your parents for the reasonable value of the support furnished to you. The right of reimbursement applies not only to money, but to food, lodging, clothing, medical care and medicines, tuition at school, and lawyer's fees for the defense of civil and criminal proceedings. It is usually limited to those items which are properly classified as "necessaries," and your father would not ordinarily be liable for the cost of an automobile furnished to you for pleasure, although he might be liable for the reasonable cost of an automobile furnished to permit you to drive to school or college or to a hospital or doctor for necessary medical treatments. Moreover your father's liability will be limited to reasonable amounts, and it obviously would be unreasonable to expect a man earning a hundred dollars a week to pay for a one-hundred-fifty-dollar suit for a seventeen-year-old boy. On the other hand, the father would be liable for several pairs of trousers, shirts, shoes and a jacket purchased at a department store at its usual prices, since these items would be within the father's means.

The age at which your father ceases to be liable for your support also varies in different states and communities, and with your father's circumstances, as well as your own. If you go to work at sixteen and earn enough to support yourself, your father will not be required to support you. If your earnings are not quite enough for your support, but are still of some assistance to you, your father will be required to furnish less, but will be required to make up the difference between what you earn and the amount reasonably necessary for your support and subsistence.

If your father is deceased, or his whereabouts are not known, or if he is disabled, and both of your grandfathers are living, the cost of your support will be divided between them. The division may be an equal one, or it may be apportioned in accordance with their means, with the more affluent grandfather bearing a larger part of the burden. If no relative can be found, the state, county, or community will assume the burden of your support, sometimes in an institution, and at other times by placing you in a foster home, and paying the foster parents a stated sum each month.

Duty of Minors to Support Children and Spouses

If you are a young man who has not yet reached his majority but nevertheless has decided to take a wife, by that act you have assumed the obligation to support her. A husband, regardless of his age, is bound by law to support his wife in accordance with his property and earning ability, honestly exercised, whether his wife is a millionaire or a pauper. It is true that in recent years courts enforcing the obligations of support have taken a more realistic viewpoint and have been somewhat more lenient in determining the amount to be paid by husbands of wealthy wives, but the general principle still applies, and the fact that you are a minor does not exempt you from the obligation to support your wife. If you are a wife, your marriage will ordinarily transfer from your father to your husband the obligation and duty to furnish you with support, but if your husband is unable to support you, you may then look to your father or grandfather, and he will ordinarily be ordered to support you.

If you become a parent before you reach the age of twenty-one, you become liable for the support of your child, not only from the moment of his birth, but also from the moment his mother becomes pregnant. You are liable for all prenatal care, whether or not you are married to the mother or expectant mother, and for all expenses of the birth, including physicians' and nurses' charges, and reasonable hospital expenses.

If you are the mother of a child, and the father cannot be

found or his obligation cannot be enforced, you yourself are responsible for the support of your child, and are answerable to persons furnishing support.

If you become the father or mother of a child born to you out of wedlock, the fact that you are a minor will not exempt you from the duty of support. Generally speaking, the primary obligation for support is cast upon the father, but in practice the obligation is enforced against both parents by in effect reducing the amount which the father is obliged to furnish the mother for the support of the child.

If you are a young man and are charged or accused by a young woman of being the father either of a child born to her, or a child which she expects, you will be entitled to a hearing or trial. If you are adjudged, after a trial, to be the father of the child, an amount will be assessed by the Court, and you will be directed to pay this amount each week or month until your child either reaches a stated age (usually eighteen, but varying in different states), or until your child dies or marries. Amounts ordered for the support of children vary from three or four dollars a week to as much as seventy-five dollars a week and sometimes more.

Support by Minors of Persons other than Spouses and Children

In most states you will be liable for the support of your parents or grandparents, if they are likely to become a public charge, and if your income, even as a minor, is sufficient to permit you to support your own immediate dependents (wife and children), and to have anything left with which to make a contribution. You may also be liable for a younger brother or sister and occasionally for a nephew or niece if your earnings or property, despite your youth, are substantial. It is best to consult a lawyer in your own community.

Public officials at times are somewhat relentless in attempting to enforce the obligation of support, and the fact that you are a minor will not relieve you of the obligation to make whatever contribution you can afford toward the support of a blood relative who is destitute and likely to become a burden on the community.

Different Types of Guardians

Until you reach your majority you are an infant, and as a minor you may act legally only with the intervention of your guardian. This is true even in States where you are allowed to vote before you attain your majority and in States where you are allowed to make a will of real or personal property before attaining your majority. While you may make a will in some states (see Chapter 5) before celebrating your majority, you may or may not buy or sell real property or any particularly valuable personal property and you may not sue as a plaintiff or be sued as a defendant in any civil lawsuit without the intervention and assistance of your guardian.

Your guardian may be of several categories. For instance, he may be a guardian only of your person, taking care of the supervision of where you live, how you behave, what medical services are rendered to you, what clothing is furnished to you, and when you are to be disciplined. He is called the guardian of your person and he has your general custody and care until he is relieved by a court order or until you attain your majority. He need not necessarily be the person having charge of your property. If he is designated as the "Guardian of the Person and Property of John Jones, an Infant" he will have the stewardship of your property as well as having your custody, but if he is merely the guardian of your person, some other person appointed by the court or by the Will of your last surviving parent may serve as the guardian of your property.

The guardian of your person has the duty of controlling you, and has the right to discipline you, to educate, feed, and house you, to tend you in illness and to provide for your recreation. In short, he may have all of the duties and rights normally belonging to a parent. As a general practice, courts do not like to appoint one person as guardian of the person of an infant and another as guardian of his property, but there are instances in which it might be advantageous. For example, you may have an aunt, or a friend of one of your parents as the guardian of your person, and a bank or trust company as the guardian of your property. The guardian of your person must be a natural person, while the guardian of your property may be either a natural person or a corporation. A partnership cannot be appointed as a guardian.

The Surrogate's Court, Orphan's Court, Superior Court or Supreme Court of the jurisdiction in which you live usually exercises close supervision over the actions of a guardian, and may, if complaint is made, inquire into the extent and amount of corporal or physical punishment inflicted on the infant or minor, his training and education and his general welfare. Insofar as the guardian of your property is concerned, the court will supervise the investments of your property, its management and your general financial welfare and will require the guardian to account at regular intervals. In some States the accounting period is based on the calendar, while in others, it is at the discretion of the court. If you have a comparatively small estate, the court will not require frequent accountings, since the expense of accountings tends to devour a large part of your income and capital. On the other hand, if you have an extremely large estate, more than you can spend, the court may require frequent accountings to be sure that the property is conserved for you until you attain your majority.

As an infant, neither you nor your guardian have the freedom of investment which you will have once you attain your adulthood. Investments in behalf of infants are limited to "legals" or "legal investments," securities which pay a lower rate of interest than common stocks or even preferred stocks but which are considered safer, and which do not have the danger of fluctuation of some of the securities having a higher income or yield.

The guardian of your property is responsible for the payment from your income and property of your debts and reasonable charges incurred for your support, maintenance and education, for the collection of debts and claims due to you, and for the investment of your property. If he does not make investments which are sufficiently profitable, as for example, if he invests in securities paying only one percent while Government Bonds paying two and a half percent are available and are considered equally safe or safer, the court may penalize him by "surcharging" and by directing him to make good to you for the balance. If without taking reasonable precautions he invested in a mortgage or in bonds which depreciated greatly in value, the court may surcharge him, and order him to make good the loss.

68

Choice of a Guardian

In selecting a guardian of your person, your mother or father may provide by Will for the designation of a certain relative or friend. This designation is not iron-clad and neither you, as the infant, nor the court which supervises your guardianship, are bound if it should appear to be adverse to your interests or if the designation of another person will be more to your advantage. Usually your parents will designate someone fairly close to you, but if they designate a relative with whom you are not on intimate terms, some other relative may intervene and the court will consider all factors before determining the person to whom your custody is to be awarded. The court may even divide your guardianship by giving the person designated in the Will the custody of your property and giving another person the custody of your person.

The power to appoint a guardian varies from state to state, and where there is likelihood of a lengthy proceeding before the court, or where there are circumstances amounting to an emergency, a court may appoint a temporary guardian until final determination can be made. Generally speaking, a general guardian (a guardian both of the person and property) will be appointed only if you, as the minor concerned, reside within the jurisdiction where the court sits. Otherwise the proceeding will, as a general rule, be transferred to the courts of your residence. In some cases, however, your mere physical presence within the state is sufficient to give the court jurisdiction regardless of the place where the court is located. However, all courts follow the general rule that in appointing a guardian their primary consideration is the welfare of the minor.

Some states permit infants over the age of fourteen to nominate their own guardians and while such guardianship is subject to approval by the court, your choice will have a decided influence on the court. Until you have attained the age of sixteen, you usually do not have the final say as to where or the persons with whom you shall live, but your wishes will be considered. Your living expenses usually are paid from your income, and not from the principal of your estate, but if money has been left to you by Will and your parents or the person responsible for your support does not have sufficient money to pay your college or technical school tuition or to provide for extraordinary medical or surgical care (such as a corrective operation), the court may permit the withdrawal of such funds from your property. All of this, however, may be done only by court order.

Guardian Ad Litem and for Purposes of Lawsuit

As long as you are an infant or a minor, you have no standing in court without the assistance of a guardian. If you operate an automobile, either your own or one belonging to someone else, and inflict personal injury or property damage upon another person, you, as well as the owner of the automobile, may be subject to suit. A lawsuit may be started against you by the service of a summons without the injured person knowing or caring whether you are an infant. Once it appears to the court that you have not attained your majority, you may not conduct the lawsuit yourself but it will be necessary for a "Guardian ad Litem" or "Guardian for Purposes of the Lawsuit" be appointed for you. This Guardian ad Litem will usually be your father or mother but if no such relative is available, it may even be the attorney who appears in the lawsuit for you. If you yourself do not make the application for the appointment of a Guardian ad Litem, the people suing you, once they discover that you are an infant, may make the application and leave it up to the court to appoint someone for you. The general procedure is for the opposing side to move for the appointment of a Guardian ad Litem and if your lawyer does not come forward with the name of some adult relative to serve as your guardian, he may find himself appointed guardian for the purposes of the lawsuit. A Guardian ad Litem may be appointed even though you have a general guardian and even though you are living with your mother and father.

If you yourself are injured in an accident, or if you have a claim against someone for a willful or intentional wrong, you must ask the court to appoint a guardian before you will be permitted to appear in court. As a rule, either your mother or your father will be appointed as Guardian ad Litem for purposes of bringing the lawsuit. A practice widely followed is to have your mother appointed as Guardian ad Litem to sue in your behalf, and to have your father join as a party plaintiff (bringing the lawsuit to recover money from another person), since as your father he is responsible for all medical bills and for your convalescent and medical care. The title of the lawsuit, therefore, generally will be as follows: "William Jones, an infant over the age of fourteen years, by Mary Jones, his Guardian ad Litem, and John Jones,

Plaintiffs

-against-
Robert Smith and the Smith Corporation,

Defendants."

You are not permitted to pursue a lawsuit in your own name until you have attained your majority, and it is necessary for the court to appoint a Guardian ad Litem to represent you. This is true in any type of lawsuit, whether in Surrogate's Court, in County Court, Superior Court or Supreme Court, to recover on a contract or on a tort, or in an action for a divorce or annulment and the rule applies whether you are the plaintiff (the person bringing the suit), or the defendant (the person against whom the suit is grought), or merely a party who is ordered to show cause why the Will of a certain relative should not be admitted to probate, or why the title to certain real property should not be declared free and clear of all liens and encumbrances.

Settlement of Claims of Minors

Until you attain your majority you are not entitled to settle a lawsuit or claim without the approval of the court. In all states young men do not first attain their majority until they complete their twenty-first year. The rule applies for young women except in Arkansas, Idaho, Illinois, Montana, North Dakota, Oklahoma, South Dakota and Utah, where young women attain their majority upon the completion of their eighteenth year.

If a lawsuit is begun in your behalf while you are a minor, it may not be settled during your minority without the specific approval of the court. Once you attain your majority your guardian ad Litem may be discharged and the lawsuit may be continued in your name. If you are over fourteen years of age your consent usually will be required, but if you are under fourteen, the court will be guided as a rule by the report of your guardian and your parents and by the attorney who represents you and your parents.

If you have a valid claim and it is to be compromised, the compromise may be effected only with the approval of the court.

In the ordinary lawsuit between adult parties, a settlement may be made at any stage of the lawsuit without the approval of the court. Where a minor is involved, however, the court will scrutinize the settlement carefully to be sure that the minor is not imposed upon and that his rights are protected. The procedure for the settlement of an infant's claim sometimes takes several months, since all parties must be scrupulous to protect the infant.

The usual procedure, after you, as a minor, are injured in an accident or the subject of a willful wrong, will be for your mother or father to consult a lawyer. The lawyer will then prepare a petition to be signed by your mother or your father, and if you are over the age of fourteen years, by you as well. If you are under the age of fourteen years, your consent is not necessary. Let us assume that you are seventeen years of age and have been struck by an automobile as you were crossing the street with a green traffic light in your favor. While you were still in the hospital, your father may have consulted an attorney and the papers will have been prepared for the appointment of your mother as your Guardian ad Litem. Your mother will then sign a petition asking a judge of the court to appoint her as your guardian to permit you to bring a lawsuit to recover for the injuries which you received. Your written consent is required as well as an affidavit from your mother that she has sufficient money to pay any damages which may be incurred by her negligence. The petition is then presented to the court, which will appoint your mother as guardian. In some cases a bond may be required to insure your protection, but ordinarily the lawsuit may be begun and the guardian appointed without the necessity of a bond. Your father will join in the lawsuit as the person responsible for your medical care, treatment and rehabilitation up to the end of your minority.

Let us suppose that as the lawsuit progresses, the owner and operator of the automobile and his insurance company realize that you are free from fault and that your injuries were sustained solely because of the negligence and carelessness of the owner and operator of the automobile. Let us assume further that you incurred medical bills of three hundred dollars and a hospital bill of four hundred dollars and that you have made a substantial recovery with the only aftereffects of your injuries being a few scars on your legs which ordinarily will be covered by your clothing.

Let us further assume that your lawyer feels that five thousand dollars is a fair settlement.

Your lawyer will then prepare a petition asking the court to approve a settlement for five thousand dollars. He will ask the court to fix his fee and will also prepare an affidavit to be signed by him stating that he believes the settlement is the best which can be obtained under the circumstances and that he believes it to be fair and adequate. If he cannot in good conscience execute this affidavit, the court will not permit the settlement of the case. He must also state that he has no connection with the people whom you are suing or with their insurance company or attorneys, and your father must also sign an affidavit and swear to the fact that he has no interest adverse to you and that he believes the settlement to be fair, reasonable and adequate.

After these papers are approved, it will be necessary for you, your lawyer and your father to appear in court before the judge. In some circumstances the judge may feel that the settlement is not enough and he will not approve it unless it is increased. If the defendant or his insurance company does not want to increase the amount, the case will then be sent back for trial and if the amount of the offer is increased, the case can be settled if the judge feels that the new offer is fair, reasonable and adequate.

At the time the judge approves the settlement he will also fix the fees of your attorney. The settlement usually will be divided into two parts, one part for you and the second part for your father, to reimburse him for the monies which he has been required to spend and which he may be required to spend in the future for your medical care, treatment, rehabilitation and medication. In some instances the judge may feel that a larger part of the settlement should be allocated to you and a smaller part to your father and he will require complete substantiation and verification of all hospital, doctor and medical bills before approving a settlement which gives an apparently disproportionate amount to your father.

Once your lawsuit is settled, you have no further redress and if there is any possibility of permanent injury the Judge will scrutinize the report very carefully and refuse to approve the settlement. In some instances he may even appoint an impartial person, either a lawyer or a doctor, to make a further examination and report. If there is any doubt as to the permanency of your injury and the adequacy of the settlement, the Judge may also appoint a Special Guardian or independent lawyer to report and to confirm the statements made by your own lawyer and your father. Occasionally parents feel that they are entitled to a larger share of the settlement, but Courts are scrupulous in safeguarding your rights as an infant, and in limiting your parents' share to their actual expenses.

After the settlement is approved and the money is paid, you will seldom receive any substantial part of it before you reach your majority. It usually will be ordered placed on deposit in a savings bank in the name of your Guardian and an Executive or Trust Officer of the savings bank, with withdrawals allowed only after the Court has given its permission. This is done not only to prevent you from squandering the money or making improper use of it, but to be sure that you receive a regular income and increment from interest, and to have the money available to you both for educational purposes or to permit you to obtain a start in life on attaining your majority. If, for example, you were sufficiently fortunate to be admitted to a medical school prior to attaining your majority, or if you wanted to attend an advanced college course, you could apply to the Court for permission to withdraw an amount sufficient for your tuition. Ordinarily you will not be permitted to withdraw money for living expenses, since these are to be furnished to you by your parents or guardian. If you are attending school and want to buy a car to travel back and forth, or if you are approaching your majority and want to get married, the Court will probably approve reasonable withdrawals to permit you to take these important steps.

The procedure for withdrawal of money varies from state to state, but as a general rule you file in Court a sworn statement asking that you be permitted to withdraw part of your money, and stating what use you intend to make of it. The Court may grant all or only part of your request, and will then sign an Order permitting the bank to let you make the withdrawal. You may rest assured, however, that you will not be permitted to withdraw the money without a very good reason.

Once you have attained your majority, the guardianship ceases and the Court will make an Order, on your request, releasing such funds to you, unless special circumstances such as your complete disability or mental incompetence arise, the guardianship will terminate when you reach your majority.

Chapter Ten

YOUTH AND MARRIAGE, DIVORCE AND ANNULMENT

Marriage is an institution so solemn and sacred and so important to the state that minors are granted special protection and consideration. Both for the protection of minors and for the welfare of the state, minimum ages for marriage have been established in all jurisdictions. There are two categories of minimum age:

1. The age at which you may marry without the necessity of obtaining the consent of your parents (Table VI-A). Until you have attained the age set forth in this table, you may not marry without the consent of your parents, and a marriage license may not be issued to you in the absence of such consent.

2. The age at which you may marry only after obtaining parental consent, and furnishing such consent to the authority charged with issuing marriage licenses. Table VI-B gives the minimum ages at which marriage may be solemnized only after parental consent has been obtained.

As is obvious from Table VI-A, the age at which you may marry without the consent of your parents varies from state to state, but in most states it has been fixed at twenty-one for men and eighteen for women. Your own state requirements are set forth in the table. Once you have attained the age set forth in Table VI-A, you may marry without the consent of your parents. Below that age, however, there is a second minimum age at which you may marry only if your parents give their consent. As you can see in Table VI-B this age also varies from state to state.

TABLE VI-A

AGES AT WHICH MARRIAGE MAY BE CONTRACTED
WITHOUT PARENTAL CONSENT

State	Age-Male	Age-Female	State	Age-Male	Age-Female
Alabama	21	18	Montana	21	21
Alaska	21	18	Nebraska	21	18
Arizona	21	18	Nevada	21	18
Arkansas	21	18	New Hampshire	20	18
California	21	18	New Jersey	21	18
Colorado	21	18	New Mexico	21	18
Connecticut	21	18	New York	21	18
Delaware	21	18	North Carolina	18	18
Dist. of Columbia	21	18	North Dakota	21	18
Florida	21	18	Ohio	21	21
Georgia	17	18	Oklahoma	21	18
Hawaii	20	20	Oregon	21	18
Idaho	18	18	Pennsylvania	21	21
Illinois	21	18	Puerto Rico	21	21
Indiana	21	18	Rhode Island	21	21
Iowa	21	18	South Carolina	18	18
Kansas	21	18	South Dakota	21	21
Kentucky	21	21	Tennessee	18	18
Louisiana	18	18	Texas	21	18
Maine	21	18	Utah	21	18
Maryland	21	18	Vermont	21	21
Massachusetts	21	18	Virginia	21	21
Michigan	18	18	Washington	21	21
Minnesota	21	18	West Virginia	21	21
Mississippi	21	18	Wisconsin	21	18
Missouri	21	18	Wyoming	21	21

In many states, the minimum age set forth in Table VI-B is not absolute, and may be waived or suspended, in your particular case, if the County Court, Surrogate's Court or Superior Court signs an order permitting the marriage. If your state is marked with a single asterisk (*), and you have not yet attained

(Text continued on p. 79.)

TABLE VI-B

AGES BELOW WHICH MINORS ARE PROHIBITED
FROM MARRYING

State	Age-Male	Age-Female	State	Age-Male	Age-Female
Alabama	17	14	Missouri	15*	15*
Alaska	18	16	Montana	18	16
Arizona	18	16*	Nebraska	18	16
Arkansas	18	16	Nevada	18	16
California	18	16	New Hampshire	14	13
Colorado	16*	16*	New Jersey	18*	16*
Connecticut	16*	16*	New Mexico	18	16
Delaware	18	16	New York	16	14
Dist. of Columbia	16	16	North Carolina	16**	16**
Florida	18**	16**	North Dakota	18	15
Georgia	17	14	Ohio	18**	15**
Hawaii	18	15	Oklahoma	18**	15**
Idaho	15	16*	Oregon	18	15
Illinois	18	16	Pennsylvania	16*	16*
Indiana	18	16	Puerto Rico	18	16
Iowa	16	14	Rhode Island	18	16
Kansas	18*	16*	South Carolina	18	14
Kentucky	16	14	South Dakota	18	15
Louisiana	18*	16*	Tennessee	16*	16*
Maine	16*	15*	Texas	16	14
Maryland	18**	18**	Utah	16	14
Massachusetts	14	12	Vermont	16	16
Michigan	18**	18**	Virginia	18**	16**
Minnesota	15	18	Washington	18	16
Mississippi	no minimum	no minimum	West Virginia	18	16
			Wisconsin	18	15
			Wyoming	18	16

---

* See text pages 77 and 79.

** Marriages contracted by persons under these ages are valid if no lawsuit is brought to have the marriage annulled, and the parties live together, or if the wife gives birth to a child before reaching the age indicated.

the age below which you are not permitted to marry even with the consent of your parents, you nevertheless may be permitted to marry if, with the consent of your parents, you show the court, by a sworn written statement, or sworn testimony in court, upon which you may be cross-examined, that you have a good reason why the minimum age requirement should be waived. If your state is marked with a double asterisk (**), you may be permitted to marry, below the minimum age, if you and your prospective spouse either are the parents of a child, or if medical tests prove to the satisfaction of the judge of the appropriate court that you are about to become the parents of a child. You should keep in mind, however, that the mere fact that you and your prospective spouse are expecting a child does not mean that the court will automatically give you permission to marry. Such permission will be granted only when the judge is convinced that the marriage is absolutely necessary for your welfare, and for the welfare of your child. Under some circumstances, for instance, if one of the parties, even at the tender age below the minimum legal age of consent, has a bad record as a criminal or juvenile delinquent, has been involved in extra-marital relationships with one or more persons other than his or her proposed spouse or is suffering from an infectious or chronic disease, or if there is doubt of the paternity of the child which is expected, the judge may, in the exercise of his discretion, refuse to grant the permission and in effect forbid the marriage, or direct its postponement.

Annulment for Non-Age

If you marry before you reach the minimum age (as shown in Table VI-B), your marriage may be declared void if you do not continue to live with your spouse after you have attained the age at which you may marry without parental consent. If you were below the minimum age (as shown in Table VI-B) and have not yet attained that minimum age, you may have the marriage declared null and void. Once you pass the age of consent, however, it will be much more difficult for you to obtain an annulment if it appears to the court that you have actually lived with your spouse, or co-habited with him or her after attaining the age of consent. If you have discontinued cohabitation before reaching the age of consent, and have not lived with your spouse since reaching such age, you may apply for an annulment, even if you wait several years, although the court will be more inclined to grant the annulment if you do not let too much time go by. Since the laws of the various states differ somewhat in this regard, it is better to consult a lawyer in the state in which you live. Some states may permit an annulment even after five years, while in other states a delay of six months may bar the relief which you seek.

If you have not yet attained your majority, and want to obtain a divorce, the court will not permit you to sue in your own name, but a "guardian ad litem," or "guardian for purposes of the lawsuit" must be appointed by the court to protect you as an infant. We have seen in Chapter Nine that until you reach the age of twenty-one, it will be appointed for you in any lawsuit in which you become involved, whether you are the party who brings the suit (the plaintiff) or the party against whom the suit is brought (the defendant). In addition to the guardian ad litem, who usually is one of your parents, or an older relative, the court may appoint a "Special Guardian" to report to the Court whether the divorce, separation or annulment is in your best interests. While the "guardian ad litem" will be someone related to you or someone whom you know, the "Special Guardian" will be someone appointed by the court, and may be an absolute stranger. If the lawsuit is begun before you attain the age of twenty-one years, and you become of age while it is pending, the Special Guardian and the guardian ad litem will cease to function, and you will be permitted to continue to prosecute or defend the suit in your own name. It will remain within the discretion of the court, however, to continue the services of the Special Guardian, and his report may be considered by the court in reaching its decision.

Even though the court grants you an annulment because of non-age at the time of the marriage, it may still grant you support if you are the wife, and order you to pay support if you are the husband. In many states, when a marriage is declared void, the rights and obligations of the parties are at an end, but in many other states the court may direct that support be paid to a wife though the marriage is otherwise at an end and has been declared null and void. If the court considers that the marriage has brought about a substantial change in the status or circumstances of the wife, the husband or former husband may be ordered to furnish support in accordance with his means.

APPENDIX A

GLOSSARY OF LEGAL TERMS

Ab initio - From the beginning. Indicates that a transaction was not valid from the time it was made. Thus a contract signed by a minor might be one that was never valid or enforceable.

Abandonment - Giving up property or a right with no intentions of ever reclaiming it again in the future. A common ground for legal separation when one spouse leaves the other without any intention to return.

Abatement - Indicates a suspension of a legal proceeding.

Abatement of nuisance - Removal of or lessening of a nuisance, whether by legal action or the individual action of the injured party.

Accord and satisfaction - A contractual agreement whereby one of the parties agrees to accept a sum of money, or less than the performance agreed upon, and thereby release the other party from further obligation under the contract.

Act of God - An inevitable accident, caused by the elements of nature. A person generally cannot be penalized for damage resulting from an Act of God.

Action - A legal proceeding, involving the assertion of one's rights against another.

Affidavit - A statement or declaration reduced to writing and sworn or affirmed before a public officer who has the power to administer an oath.

Annulment - A declaration by a court that a marriage presumed to be binding is a nullity and ineffective.

Answer - A document which the defendant in a civil lawsuit serves on the plaintiff or his attorney in answer to the summons and complaint.

Appeal - The proceeding by which a party to a lawsuit defeated in a lower court applies to a higher court to get a review of the decision in the lower court.

Appearance - The coming into court as a party to a lawsuit. The formal proceeding whereby a person submits to the jurisdiction of the court.

Arbitration - A proceeding agreed to in a previous agreement in which both parties to a controversy submit their dispute to persons designated or to be chosen.

Arraignment - The calling of the defendant in a criminal case before the court to answer the charges in the indictments and plead guilty, not guilty, or no contest.

Arrest - The legal seizure and restraint of a person charged with a crime so that he may be brought to court to stand trial.

Assignment - The transfer of a right or interest in property by one person to another.

Attachment - The taking into custody of the law of the person or property of one already before the court, or one whom it is sought to bring before the court.

Attestation Clause - The formal language used at the end of a will, below the testator's signature, which declares that the requirements for the proper execution of the will have been complied with.

Bail - Security given to a court in exchange for the release of a person in custody to assure his presence in court later.

Bail Bond - An undertaking by which someone obligates himself to pay the amount of the bail if the person out on bail fails to appear at the required time.

Bailment - The delivery of personal property by one person to another, to be held or used for some purpose, and to be returned when the purpose is fulfilled. For example, the delivery of furniture to a warehouse by the owner is a "bailment."

Bankruptcy - A proceeding under federal laws, dealing with the property and debts of an insolvent debtor and his creditors.

Bigamy - Willful contracting of a second marriage when the contracting party knows that the first marriage contract is still valid and legally binding.

Bearer Paper - Any negotiable instrument which can be negotiated by delivery and does not require endorsement.

Bill of Particulars - A document in a lawsuit which spells out the information set forth in the complaint of the plaintiff.

Binder - Used in insurance and real estate, is a preliminary agreement.

Bona Fide - Good faith, honesty, contrasted with bad faith. Used in contracts and negotiable instruments, describes any person who acquires property or negotiable instruments in good faith and for a valuable consideration.

Breach of the peace - Any act committed by a person in a public place which creates a disturbance.

Breach of Contract - The violation of an obligation or duty set forth or implied in an agreement.

Burglary - A crime committed by a person who breaks into and enters the premises of another without consent and with intent to commit a crime.

Calendar - The list of cases which is established in each court to determine their orderly disposition and trial.

Caveat Emptor - "Let the buyer beware."

Challenge - The right of a party to a lawsuit to object to a juror during the selection of the jury before the trial.

Chattel - Any property, real or personal, movable or immovable, which is less than a "Freehold."

Codicil - A document, executed with all the formality of a will, used to make minor changes in an existing will.

Common Law - The body of law which was accumulated and collected from the decisions of the English courts and adopted as the basis of law in this country.

Condemnation - The legal machinery by which an authorized governmental agency takes private property for public use.

Confrontation - The act by which a witness is brought into the presence of the accused.

Consanguinity - Persons related by blood and by descent from a common ancestor.

Consideration - The price, motive, or manner of inducement to enter into a contract. Most contracts are unenforceable unless there is consideration recognized as such by law.

Conspiracy - An agreement between two or more people to commit an illegal act, or to accomplish a legal act by illegal means.

Contempt - The disobedience of the rules, orders and processes of the court or legislative body.

Conveyance - The transfer of title to and from one person to another.

Conviction - The verdict of guilty by a jury in a criminal proceeding, or the final judgment of guilt by a court.

Creditor - One to whom money is owed.

Custody - The legal right given to a parent or another person to live with, control, educate and guide children; the care and keeping of anything.

Damages - Compensation in the form of money which may be recovered in the courts by any person who has suffered loss, detriment, or injury through the unlawful act or omission, or the negligence of someone else.

Decedent - In wills and estates is used to denote the deceased person whose estate is involved.

Decree - A formal determination of a court, usually made in writing.

Deed - A document which transfers ownership to real estate.

Defamation - A statement made orally or in writing which injures a person's reputation in the community.

Default - The omission or failure to fulfill a duty, observe a promise, discharge an obligation, or perform an agreement; a legal term meaning the failure to appear and defend a lawsuit.

Defendant - The person against whom recovery is sought in a lawsuit.

Dependent - One who derives support from another.

Deposition - A written statement made under oath.

Devise - A grant or transfer of real estate by will.

Disability - The lack of legal capacity to do a certain act.

Divorce - The dissolution of the marriage relationship by law.

Domicile - The place of permanent residence of an individual.

Due Process - The fundamental rights guaranteeing a fair trial to which every United States citizen is entitled in any legal proceeding.

Easement - The right of a landowner to use the land of his neighbor.

Ejectment - The legal remedy available to the owner of real estate to remove persons in possession who have no right to be there.

Eminent Domain - The power of the government to take property for public use. In the United States this cannot be done without just compensation to the owner of the property.

Escheat - The return of land and property to the state if there is no person legally entitled to inherit.

Estate - The property of a deceased person.

Eviction - The act which deprives a person of the possession of his property.

Ex Parte - An act accomplished in the course of legal proceedings without the presence of one of the parties.

Ex Post Facto Law - Designates an act to be a crime although it was not a crime when it was committed.

Express Contract - All provisions of the contract were agreed upon by the parties. A contract is implied when it is created by the conduct of the parties.

Extortion - The offense of taking money or property from a person by threat or duress or under pretense of authority.

False Arrest - The detention of a person by another who claims to have official authority which is in fact invalid.

False Imprisonment - Any unlawful restriction of a man's liberty.

Fiduciary - A person acting in a position of trust in relation to other persons.

Fixtures - Items of personal property which may become a part of the real property when they are attached and cannot be removed.

Foreclosure - A proceeding whereby mortgaged property is applied to pay the mortgage debt, upon the default of the debtor.

Fraud - A false statement of a material fact made to induce someone to rely upon it to his financial loss.

Garnishment - A notice or proceeding which requires a person who owes money to a judgment debtor to pay the judgment creditor instead. This is often done in the case of salary which the debtor is earning. The money is applied to the payment of the debt.

Grand Jury - A body of citizens who are called together to examine into the facts of a case to determine whether or not an indictment should be issued for criminal proceedings.

Guardian - A person appointed to be a protector of the interests of a minor.

Habeas Corpus - A legal writ demanding that a prisoner be produced at a certain time and place in order that the judge may determine the course of action to take in his behalf. The granting of the writ generally results in the release of the prisoner. This is generally used as a protection against the unwarranted arrest and detention of a person without just cause.

Hearsay Evidence - Evidence brought out by the testimony of a witness at a trial which is not based upon his personal knowledge but rather on information he obtained from someone else, someone not available for cross-examination. This evidence is generally not acceptable.

Heir - The person entitled under the law to acquire the real property of a decedent in the absence of a will.

Indenture - A formal written agreement.

Indictment - A written accusation against one or more persons, prepared by the district attorney and approved by the grand jury.

Infant - Also known as a Minor, is a person under legal age, generally 21.

Information - An accusation against a person of the commission of a criminal offense, generally by another person or by a district attorney.

Injunction - An order of a court which prohibits a named person from performing certain acts.

Insolvency - The condition of a person who is unable to pay his debts.

Intestacy - The state of dying without a will.

Judgment - The formal decision or sentence of the law, given by a court of justice as the result of the proceedings conducted therein. In a money damage case, the winner to whom money is to be paid is the Judgment Creditor. The one who owes the money is the Judgment Debtor.

Jurisdiction - The legal authority which a court has to try a lawsuit.

Larceny - The stealing of anything of value.

Lease - A contract whereby a person who owns property gives a lesser interest to someone else.

Lien - A claim which a person has against the property of another which is in his possession. He may retain the property until the debt is satisfied.

Majority - The state of a person who has reached full age, or usually 21 years.

Nominal Damages - A small sum, generally 6 cents, given when the invasion of a right is proved, but there is no indication or proof of substantial damage.

Notary Public - A person authorized under state law to administer an oath, having the power to attest writings to establish their authenticity, et. al.

Pardon - An act by the governor of a state, which releases a person convicted of a crime from punishment imposed by the sentence of a court.

Perjury - Willfully telling a falsehood under oath.

Pleading - The stating in a logical and legal form the facts which constitute the plaintiff's cause of action or the defendant's defense.

Putative Father - The father of an illegitimate child.

Quantum Meruit - "amount deserved" is the relief in money which is awarded to a plaintiff in an action based on a contract implied by law.

Ratification - An agreement to adopt as one's own the act performed by another.

Satisfaction of Judgment - A document which states that a recorded judgment has been paid and satisfied.

Solvency - The excess of assets over liabilities. The condition of a person who is able to pay his debts out of present means.

Squatter - A person who takes possession of land without any claim or color of title.

Statute of Limitations - A series of legal provisions which limit the time when a plaintiff may bring a lawsuit.

Subpoena - The process by which the attendance of a witness is required at a proceeding.

Summons -- The process by which a case is brought before the court by advising the defendant that there is a claim against him.

Surety - The person who promises to make good the obligation of another.

Surrogate - The judge who presides in the court where estates of deceased persons are administered.

Title - The ownership in property.

Tort - A legal wrong, done by one person to another.

Trespass - The act of coming upon the land of another without permission; an unlawful interference with the rights of another, accompanied by force, either actually or implied by law.

Usury - Unlawful interest beyond the rate established by law.

Venue - The court which has jurisdiction to try a case.

Waiver - The act of giving up a right which a person has.

Warrant - A process of a criminal court which authorizes search or seizure of persons or property.

Writ - a process of a court ordering a public officer or a private person to do a certain act.

APPENDIX B

UNIFORM NARCOTICS DRUG ACT (Excerpts)

An Act defining and relating to narcotic drugs and to make uniform the law with reference thereto.

Note: The Uniform Narcotics Act has been adopted by most of the states although the penalty provisions, left blank in the recommended Act, vary from state to state. Furthermore, in many states, as well as in some municipalities, special measures have been enacted aimed particularly at addicts. Addiction, for example, has been declared to be a crime in itself in some states and in others it has been included in the definitions of vagrancy and disorderly behavior. Some states also have "needle laws" which make it a punishable offense for addicts to have in their possession the paraphernalia required to make an injection.

#1. Definitions

The following words and phrases, as used in this act, shall have the following meanings, unless the context otherwise requires:

. . . . . .

(10) "Sale" includes barter, exchange or gift, or offer therefor, and each transaction made by any person, whether as principal, proprietor, agent, servant, or employee.

. . . .

(14) "Narcotic drugs" mean coca leaves, opium, cannabis, and every other substance neither chemically nor physically distinguishable from them; any other drugs to which the Federal Narcotic Laws may not apply; and any drug found by the (State Commissioner of Health or other competent officer), after reasonable notice and opportunity for hearing, to have an addiction-forming or addiction-sustaining liability similar to morphine or cocaine, from the effective date of determination of such finding by said (State Commissioner of Health or other competent state officer).

(15) "Federal Narcotic Laws" mean the laws of the United States relating to opium, coca leaves, and other narcotic drugs.

. . . .

(17) "Dispense" includes distribute, leave with, give away, dispose of, or deliver.

. . . .

#2. Acts Prohibited.

It shall be unlawful for any person to manufacture, possess, have under his control, sell, prescribe, administer, dispense, or compound any narcotic drug, except as authorized by this act.

#3. Manufacturers and Wholesalers.

No person shall manufacture, compound, mix, cultivate, grow, or by any other process produce or prepare narcotic drugs, and no person as a wholesaler shall supply the same, without having first obtained a license from the (insert here the proper official designation of state officer or board).

#4. Qualifications for Licenses.

. . . .

#5. Sale on Written Orders.

. . . .

#6. Sale by Apothecaries.

. . . . . .

#7. Professional Use of Narcotic Drugs.

. . . . . .

#8. Preparations Exempted.

. . . . . .

#9. Record to be Kept.

. . . . . .

#10. Labels.

. . . . . .

#11. Authorized Possession of Narcotic Drugs by Individuals.

A person to whom or for whose use any narcotic drug has been prescribed, sold, or dispensed, by a physician, dentist, apothecary, or other person authorized under the provisions of Section 5 of this act, and the owner of any animal for whom any drug has been prescribed, sold, or dispensed, by a veterinarian, may lawfully possess it only in the container in which it was delivered to him by the person selling or dispensing the same.

#12. Persons and Corporations Exempted.

. . . . . .

#13. Common Nuisances.

Any store, shop, warehouse, dwelling house, building, vehicle, boat, aircraft, or any place whatever, which is resorted to by narcotic drug addicts for the purpose of using narcotic drugs or which is used for the illegal keeping or selling of the same, shall be deemed a common nuisance. No person shall keep or maintain such a common nuisance.

#14. Narcotic Drugs to be Delivered to State Officials, etc.

. . . . . .

#15. Notice of Conviction to be Sent to Licensing Board.

. . . .

#16. Records Confidential.

. . . .

#17. Fraud or Deceit.

(1) No person shall obtain or attempt to obtain a narcotic drug, or procure or attempt to procure the administration of a narcotic drug, (a) by fraud, deceit, misrepresentation, or subterfuge; or (b) by the forgery or alteration of a prescription or of any written order; or (c) by the concealment of a material fact; or (d) by the use of a false name or giving a false address.

(2) Information communicated to a physician in an effort unlawfully to procure a narcotic drug, or unlawfully to procure the administration of any such drug, shall not be deemed a privileged communication.

(3) No person shall willfully make a false statement in any prescription, order, report, or record, required by this act.

(4) No person shall, for the purpose of obtaining a narcotic drug, falsely assume the title of, or represent himself to be, a manufacturer, wholesaler, apothecary, physician, dentist, veterinarian, or other authorized person.

(5) No person shall make or utter any false or forged prescription or false or forged written order.

(6) No person shall affix any false or forged label to a package or receptacle containing narcotic drugs.

. . . .

#18. Exceptions and Exemptions not Required to be Negated.

. . . .

#19. Enforcement and Cooperation.

. . . .

#20. Penalties.

. . . .

#21. Effect of Acquittal or Conviction under Federal Narcotics Laws.

FEDERAL LAWS

The legislative control of the federal government over narcotics and dangerous drugs rests in the following laws enacted in the last 60 years.

(a) Harrison Narcotics Act (1914)

A tax measure designed to control the importation, manufacture, production, preparation, purchase, sale, distribution, or gift of opium and its derivatives. It requires registration and payment of an occupational tax of all who deal in these substances. Prior to this act, opium and its derivatives could be purchased at drug stores without prescription. The act limits sales or transfers to registrants using official order forms, allowing exceptions only for legitimate medical or dental practice. Federal courts have maintained that dispensing of drugs to an addict merely for the gratification of addiction is not legitimate medical or dental practice.

(b) Narcotics Drugs Import and Export Act (1922)

This is a reenactment and revision of an earlier law. It

limits the importation of crude opium and coca leaves to amounts deemed necessary for medical and scientific needs and specifically prohibits the importation of opium for smoking or for the manufacture of heroin. The purpose of this act is to stamp out the use of narcotics in the United States except for legitimate purposes.

(c) Marijuana Tax Act (1937)

The controls over marijuana provided by this legislation are similar to those over opium provided by the Harrison Narcotics Act. The same exceptions are allowable for medical practice, but these are academic today because the medical use of marijuana is obsolete. This act, therefore, suppresses the use of marijuana in this country.

(d) Opium Poppy Control Act (1942)

Prohibits the production of the opium poppy in the United States except under license and provides penalties for persons who grow the poppy illegally.

(e) Boggs Act (1951)

A mandatory-sentence act which provides severe penalties for the illegal possession or sale of narcotics drugs and limits the suspension of sentences or the granting of probation or parole.

(f) Narcotic Control Act (1956)

Resulted from intensive studies made by Senate and House Committees which investigated the narcotics problem in the United States in the wake of the postwar increase in juvenile addiction. Both committees recommended the imposition of heavy penalties as the strongest known deterrent to narcotic traffic and narcotic addiction.

This act provides as penalty for the unlawful sale of narcotics or marijuana between adults (first offense) a sentence of not less than five nor more than 20 years, with an optional fine of up to $20,000. No probation, suspension, or parole is allowed. For the adult who in any manner furnishes heroin to a minor, the act pro-

vides for imprisonment from ten years to life, for optional fine
up to $20,000, or for the death penalty if the injury so directs.

(g) Drug Abuse Control Amendments of 1965

The Drug Abuse Control Amendments to the Federal Food,
Drug, and Cosmetic Act apply to depressant and stimulant drugs,
other than the narcotics, and to other drugs which are determined
to have a potential for abuse because of their depressant, stimulant, or hallucinogenic effect on man. Barbiturates, amphetamine,
LSD, and comparable drugs are included under these provisions,
and other drugs may be added as the need arises. These amendments place strict controls over the illegal manufacture, distribution, possession, or prescription of these drugs and increase
the enforcement powers of the Food and Drug Administration in-
spectors in dealing with infringements of the law.

APPENDIX C
JURY SERVICE

Excerpt from A Handbook of Information for Trial Jurors Serving in the Courts of the Counties of New York and the Bronx

----

IMPORTANCE OF JURY SERVICE

Trial by jury is one of the cornerstones of judicial administration. Under our American system of administering justice the persons who compose the jury are a part of the Court itself. Your work, therefore, is as important as the work of the judge who presides at the trial. Because of this importance, jury service is one of the highest duties of citizenship.

The cases which require your services involve disputes of fact. Your duty as a juror is to consider carefully the evidence presented in the case and to determine the true facts. To these facts you must then apply the law as defined to you by the judge.

Sound judgment, absolute integrity, and complete impartiality are expected of you as a juror. Remember that each case in which you sit is a matter of grave importance to the parties involved. If you are to fulfill your obligation as a juror under the oath which you will take, you should render the same thoughtful consideration and attention that you would expect from a jury in a case in which you were a party.

LITIGANTS AND PLEADING

The party who commences the lawsuit is called the plaintiff. In criminal cases the State of New York is always the plaintiff. The party against whom the action is brought is called the defendand. A party may be an individual or may be a firm or corporation.

The plaintiff's claim is asserted in a complaint. The defendant gives his defense in an answer. Sometimes a defendant asserts a claim against the plaintiff. This is called a counter claim. These papers are called pleadings. Thus, each party has a right to be informed of his adversary's claim against him.

It is in this general way that the issues are clearly defined for presentation to the court, and to you, as jurors, for a verdict, based on your search for the truth.

PROCEDURE IN CIVIL CASES

The trial begins with the selection of jurors. In order that a completely impartial jury may be selected, prospective jurors will be questioned either by the judge or by the attorneys. You should answer their questions frankly and accurately, bearing in mind that their purpose is to determine whether any prospective juror should be excused from participating in the case. The law also permits the attorney for each party to "challenge" a certain number of jurors without assigning any specific reason for doing so. If you are so "challenged," you should not feel that this is done on any personal basis nor to secure any unfair advantage to any party. It involves no reflection whatever upon the juror so excused.

After you have been selected to participate in a particular case as a juror, you are required to take a solemn oath that you will "well and truly try the issues and render a true verdict according to the evidence."

The examination and selection of jurors in civil cases is often conducted by counsel outside the court room, either in the juror's assembly room or in an adjoining room. This is done to conserve the judge's time so that he may proceed with other judicial business while your jury is being impanelled, but he always maintains supervision over the impanelling of the panel.

Ordinarily the jury is composed of 12 persons. However, the parties have the option of proceeding with a jury of 6 persons. Where a trial is likely to be protracted, "alternate," or additional, jurors may be selected, so that a substitute will be available should one of the regular jurors become ill during the course of the trial.

Upon the opening of the case, the attorney for the plaintiff presents to the judge and the jury a statement of the facts upon which the plaintiff intends to rely in order to succeed. The attorney for the defendant then states his client's position in opposition. The opening statements by the lawyers for the respective parties are not evidence. They are merely outlines of what each side hopes to prove. Their purpose is to enable you to follow the evidence more easily.

The evidence, oral or documentary, is then presented for the jury's consideration by the respective attorneys under the supervision of the judge. After all of the evidence has been received, arguments are made by the attorneys of both parties.

The judge will then deliver his instructions, commonly referred to as a "charge," to the jury. The purpose of the "charge" is to inform the jury of the law which must be applied to the various factual determinations which the jury may reach.

After the judge has delivered his "charge" the jurors retire to a place of privacy for their deliberations. It is the duty of the foreman of the jury to see that the deliberations are carried on in an orderly fashion. In reaching its verdict the jury should first determine the truth of the factual matters in dispute and then apply the proper law as "charged" by the judge. When the jury reaches its decision it returns to the courtroom and announces its verdict through the jury foreman to the judge.

The verdict in a civil case requires the agreement of at least five-sixths of the jurors; ten jurors when the jury is composed of twelve persons, and five jurors when the jury is composed of six persons.

PROCEDURE IN CRIMINAL CASES

The laws of this state require that the defendant in a criminal case be indicted by a Grand Jury or be named in an information filed by the District Attorney or other prosecutor before he can be made to stand trial.

An indictment is a written complaint voted by a majority of the members of the Grand Jury after having heard only evidence presented by the District Attorney. Neither an indictment nor an information is evidence in the case or proof of guilt. It is merely the legal means by which the defendant is brought before the court. It is the evidence at the trial which alone may be considered by the jury.

In all jury cases with which you as a juror are concerned, the defendant has answered the charge of the indictment or information by pleading "Not Guilty."

The procedure in criminal cases is similar to that in civil cases. Differences will be revealed to you in the course of the trial through your own observations and the instructions of the judge.

The jury's verdict in a criminal case is required to be unanimous.

PROCEDURE IN SURROGATE'S COURT

Jurors who are to serve in the Surrogate's Court are selected from the panel of jurors in attendance at the Supreme Court.

The jurisdiction of the Surrogate's Court pertains particularly to the estates of deceased persons. There are two types of proceedings in which juries commonly act. One is a proceeding in which the validity of a last will and testament of a deceased person is attacked, and this is known as a contested probate proceeding. The issues in such a contest ordinarily pertain to the proper signing, witnessing, and publishing of the will, the mental capacity of the decedent, and whether decedent was subjected to any improper influence or fraud.

The second type of proceeding is known as a discovery proceeding, in which the executor or the administrator, acting as the representative of a decedent's estate, endeavors to recover personal property or money which he contends belongs to the decedent's estate, which the person against whom the proceeding is brought claims the ownership of the personal property or money in dispute.

In all jury cases in the Surrogate's Court, particular questions are submitted to the jury for answer and the surrogate charges the jurors as to the applicable law with regard to the questions submitted to them.

As in other civil cases, a verdict in the Surrogate's Court requires the concurrence of ten of the twelve jurors.

APPENDIX D
BASIC LEGAL FORMS

The Appendix which follows is in the nature of an introduction to
basic legal forms. They are presented in blank, and serve only
as a guide to the types of instruments required in basic legal transactions.

Included are the following:

D-1   Form of Basic Contract

D-2   Form of Bill of Sale

D-3   Form of Bill of Sale of Motor Vehicle

D-4   Form of Lease of Apartment

D-5   Form of Deed for a Minor and Special Guardian

D-6   Form of Last Will and Testament with subscrip-
       tion clause and affidavit of subscribint witness

Since most documents require acknowledgement taken by a notary
public, forms of acknowledgement are also furnished:

D-7   Form of Acknowledgement (Individual)

D-8   Form of Acknowledgement (Corporate)

FORM OF BASIC CONTRACT

AGREEMENT ENTERED INTO BETWEEN

of the first part,

and

of the second part.
The part   of the first part, in consideration of

covenant and agree to

The part   of the second part, in consideration of

covenant and agree

This instrument may not be changed orally.

In Witness Whereof, the parties hereunto have set their hands and seals the   day of   in the year of one thousand nine hundred and

Sealed and delivered in the presence of

Acknowledgment by a notary
is optional. See Form D-7
for standard form of
acknowledgment of individual.

FORM OF BILL OF SALE

KNOW ALL MEN BY THESE PRESENT, that

of the first part, for and in consideration of the sum of

Dollars ($) lawful money of
the United States, to   in hand paid, at or before the enseal-
ing and delivery of these presents, by

of the second part, the receipt whereof is hereby acknowledged,
ha   bargained and sold, and by these presents do   grant and
convey unto the said part   of the second part   executors,
administrators and assigns,

To Have and to Hold the same unto the said part   of the
second part,   executors, administrators and assigns forever.
And   do   , for   heirs, executors and administrators, covenant and agree to and with the said part   of the second part, to
Warrant and Defend the sale of the said
hereby sold unto the said part   of the second part,   executors,
administrators and assigns, against all and every person and persons whomsoever.

In Witness Whereof: ha   hereunto set   hand   and
seal this   day of   Nineteen Hundred and

In Presence of

_____	(L.S.)
_____	(L.S.)
_____	(L.S.)
_____	(L.S.)

Acknowledgement as in
form set out at D-7

FORM OF BILL OF SALE OF MOTOR VEHICLES

KNOW ALL MEN BY THESE PRESENTS,
    That   the Seller,
whose address is
for and in consideration of the sum of $ paid by
                     the Buyer, whose address is

have bargained, sold, granted and conveyed and by these presents
do bargain, sell, grant and convey unto the Buyer, and Buyer's
successors (heirs, executors, administrators) and assigns one
Model   Factory No.   Motor No.

    To Have and to Hold the same unto the Buyer and Buyer's
successors (heirs, executors, administrators) and assigns forever, and the Seller covenants and agrees to warrant and defend
the said described motor vehicle hereby sold against all and every
person or persons whomsoever.

    The motor vehicle purports to have been operated, as ap-
pears by the odometer,   miles.

    The Seller knows that the mileage indicated on the odometer
is beyond its designed mechanical limits; the true cumulative
mileage is   miles.

    The odometer mileage is known to the Seller to be less than
the motor vehicle has travelled; the true mileage is unknown.

    The Seller also certifies that the Seller owned the vehicle
since   19   until the date of this Bill of Sale.

In Witness Whereof, the Seller has set his hand and seal or caused these presents to be signed by its proper corporate officers and caused its proper corporate seal to be hereto affixed, the day of   19   .

Signed, Sealed and Delivered   _____
    in the Presence of   (Seller)

Acknowledgement as in
form set out in D-7

FORM OF LEASE OF APARTMENT

THIS AGREEMENT, Made the   day
of   in the year one thousand nine hundred and
BETWEEN   as Landlord, and
                                    as Tenant, Witnesseth, that
the Landlord has agreed to LET, and hereby does LET, to the Tenant and the Tenant had agreed to TAKE, and hereby does TAKE
from the Landlord the   apartment on the
of the house known and designated as
in the   , Borough of   for the term of
to commence   , 19 , and to end   , 19 ,
to be occupied as a strictly private dwelling apartment by said
Tenant and his immediate family only, and not otherwise. And the
Tenant hereby covenants and agrees to pay to the Landlord the
            rent or sum of   Dollars payable
in advance in equal   payments of $ each,
on the   day of

This lease is granted upon the express condition, however,
that in case the Landlord, his agents or assigns deems objectionable or improper any conduct on the part of the Tenant or occupants, the Landlord, his agents or assigns, shall have full license
and authority to re-enter, and to have full possession of said premises, either with or without legal process, on giving five days'
previous notice of intention to do so, and tendering repayment of
the rent paid on account of the unexpired term demised; and upon
the expiration of said notice and tender of payment made as aforesaid, the Landlord, his agents or assigns, shall be entitled to the
immediate possession thereof; and in consideration of the above
letting the Tenant consents that the Landlord, his agents or assigns, shall not be liable to prosecution or damages for so resum-
ing possession of said premises.

The said premises are also Leased upon the further Covenants and Conditions:

1st.--That the Tenant shall take good care of the Apartment and fixtures, and suffer no waste or injury; shall not drive picture or other nails into the walls or woodwork of said premises, nor allow the same to be done; and shall at his own cost and expense make and do all repairs required to walls, ceilings, paper, glass and glass globes, plumbing-works, ranges, pipes and fixtures belonging thereto whenever damage or injury to the same shall have resulted from misuse or neglect; and shall repair and make good any damage occurring to the buildings, or any tenant thereof, by reason of any neglect, carelessness or injury to the dumb-waiters, gas or water pipes, meters or faucets, and connections by the Tenant himself or any of his family or household or upon the premises leased to the Tenant and not call on the Landlord for any disbursement whatsoever; and at the end or other expiration of the term, shall deliver up the demised premises in good order and condition, damage by the elements excepted; and the Landlord shall be exempt from any and all liability for any damage or injury to person or property caused by or resulting from steam, electricity, gas, water, rain, ice or snow, or any leak or flow from or into any part of said building, or from any damage or injury resulting or arising from any other cause or happening whatsoever unless said damage or injury be caused by or be due to the negligence of the Landlord.

2nd.--That the Tenant shall not expose any sign, advertisement, illumination or projection in or out of the windows or exterior, or from said building, or upon it in any place, except such as shall be approved and permitted in writing by the Landlord or his authorized agent, and the Tenant shall use only such shades in the front windows of said apartment as are put up or approved by the Landlord.

3rd.--That the Tenant, heirs, executors or administrators shall not assign this agreement, or underlet the premises, or any part thereof, or make any alterations in the apartments or premises without the Landlord's or agent's consent in writing; or permit or suffer upon the same, any act or thing deemed extra-hazardous on account of fire; and shall comply with all the rules and regulations of the Board of Health and City Ordinances applicable to said premises; and the Tenant will not use or permit to be used the said premises nor any part thereof for any purpose other than that of a private dwelling apartment for himself and his immediate family.

4th.--That the Tenant shall, in case of fire, give immediate notice thereof to the Landlord, who shall thereupon cause the damage to be repaired as soon as reasonably and conveniently may be, but if the premises be so damaged that the Landlord shall decide not to rebuild, the term shall cease, and the accrued rent be paid up to the time of the fire.

5th.--That the Tenant shall consult and conform to the regulations governing said house, and to any reasonable alteration or regulation that may be deemed necessary for the protection of the building, and the general comfort and welfare of the occupants of the same.

6th.--That in case of default in any of the covenants the Landlord may re-enter the premises, the same to have again, repossess and enjoy and the Landlord may relet the same for the remainder of the term at the best rent that he can obtain for account of the Tenant, who shall make good any deficiency; Tenant expressly waives the service of any notice in writing of intention to re-enter as provided for in any law of the State of New York and hereby waives all right of redemption to which the Tenant or any person claiming under the Tenant might be entitled by any law now or hereafter in force. In the event that the premises leased to the Tenant are vacated, the Landlord reserves the right to rent the premises for a longer period of time than fixed in the original lease without releasing the original Tenant from any liability.

7th.--That three months prior to the expiration of the term hereby granted, applicants shall be admitted at reasonable hours of the day to view the premises until rented; and the Landlord or his agents, shall also be permitted at any time during the term to visit and examine them at any reasonable hour of the day, and whenever necessary for any repairs to same or any part of the building, the Landlord, his servants and agents shall be permitted to make the same.

8th.--That where store-rooms are provided by the Landlord to accommodate tenants in the storage of different articles, it is done with the express understanding that the room is furnished gratuitously by the Landlord, and that tenants using the same do so at their own risk, and that the Landlord shall not be liable for any loss, damage, or injury whatsoever.

9th.--That in case it shall become necessary or proper at any time, from accident, or for improving the conditions or operation of the heating apparatus, plumbing, boilers, machinery, electric plant, or anything appertaining thereto, to omit the operation of said light or heating apparatus or other service, until all necessary repairs or improvements shall have been made and completed, the Landlord shall be at liberty to do the same without in any manner or respect affecting or modifying the obligations or covenants of the Tenant herein contained and in such case the Landlord shall use due expedition and diligence to repair, improve or reconstruct the same.

10th.--The Tenant has this day deposited with the Landlord the sum of $_____ as security for the full and faithful performance by the Tenant of all the terms and conditions upon the Tenant's part to be performed, which said sum shall be returned to the Tenant after the time fixed as the expiration of the term herein, provided the Tenant has fully and faithfully carried out all of the terms, covenants and conditions on the Tenant's part to be performed.

11th.--This instrument may not be changed orally.

12th.--The failure of the Landlord to insist upon a strict performance of any of the terms, conditions and covenants herein, shall not be deemed a waiver of any rights or remedies that the Landlord may have, and shall not be deemed a waiver of any subsequent breach or default in the terms, conditions and covenants herein contained.

13th.--If the leased premises, or any part thereof, are taken by virtue of eminent domain, this lease shall expire on the date when the same shall be so taken, and the rent shall be apportioned as of said date. No part of any award, however, shall belong to the tenant.

14th.--This lease shall be subject and subordinate at all times to the lien of existing mortgages and of mortgages which hereafter may be made a lien on the premises. Although no instrument or act on the part of the Tenant shall be necessary to effectuate such subordination, the Tenant will, nevertheless, execute and deliver such further instruments subordinating this lease to the lien of any such mortgages as may be desired by the mortgagee. The Tenant hereby appoints the Landlord his attorney in fact, irrevocably, to execute and deliver any such instrument for the Tenant.

15th.--Landlord shall not be liable for failure to give possession of the premises upon commencement date by reason of the fact that premises are not ready for occupancy, or due to a prior Tenant wrongfully holding over or any other person wrongfully in possession or for any other reason: in such event the rent shall not commence until possession is given or is available, but the term herein shall not be extended.

16th.--This lease and the obligations of Tenant to pay rent hereunder and perform all of the other covenants and agreements hereunder on part of Tenant to be performed shall in nowise be affected, impaired or excused because Landlord is unable to supply or is delayed in supplying any service expressly or impliedly to be supplied or is unable to make, or is delayed in making any repairs, additions, alterations or decorations or is unable to supply or is delayed in supplying any equipment or fixtures if Landlord is prevented or delayed from so doing by reason of governmental preemption in connection with any National Emergency declared by the President of the United States or in connection with any rule, order or regulation of any department or subdivision thereof of any governmental agency or by reason of the conditions of supply and demand which have been or are affected by war or other emergency.

17th.--The landlord covenants that the Tenant, on paying the rent and performing the covenants hereof, shall and may peaceably and quietly have, hold and enjoy the leased premises for the term herein mentioned.

IT IS HEREBY EXPRESSLY UNDERSTOOD AND AGREED that the character of the occupancy of said demised premises, as above expressed, is an especial consideration and inducement for the granting of this lease by the Landlord to the Tenant, and in the event of a violation by the Tenant of the restriction against subletting the premises, or permitting the same to be occupied by parties other than as aforesaid, or of a violation of any other restriction or condition therein imposed, said Lease and agreement shall, at the option of said Landlord, his agents or assigns, cease and determine and be at an end, anything hereinbefore contained to the contrary hereof in anywise notwithstanding.

In Witness Whereof, the parties to these presents have hereunto set their hands and seals, the day and year first above written.

Sealed and Delivered in the presence of

FORM OF DEED FOR A MINOR AND SPECIAL GUARDIAN

THIS INDENTURE, made this   day of   19 ,
       BETWEEN

                   , an infant,

residing at

                , County of

and State of New York, by
his Special Guardian, party of the first part, and

                part of the second part:

     WHEREAS, a petition praying for the sale of the real property hereinafter described, owned by the said infant, was presented to the   Court of the County of
on the   day of   19 , and an order of said Court was made and entered on that day appointing the above named
Special Guardian of the said infant for the purpose of the proceedings, and the said Special Guardian having on the   day
of   , 19 , duly filed his bond duly approved by this Court pursuant to the said Order.

     AND WHEREAS by an order of this Court made and entered on the   day of   , 19 ,   Esq.,
was duly appointed Referee to inquire into the merits of the application and to examine into the truth of the allegations of the petition, hear the allegations and proofs of all parties interested in the property or otherwise interested in the application and report his opinion thereon, together with the testimony, with all convenient speed,

     AND WHEREAS   , the said
Referee, did on the   day of   , 19 , duly file his report as required by law, recommending that the real property of the said infant hereinafter described be sold for not less than the sum of   Dollars,

     AND WHEREAS the said report was, by an order of said Court granted and entered on the   day of   19 , duly confirmed, and a sale of the said real property directed to be made at a sum not less than   Dollars, and requiring the said Special Guardian, before making such sale, to enter into a contract therefor subject to the approval of said Court and to report the same thereto under oath.

AND WHEREAS the said Special Guardian, pursuant to the said order, entered into a contract with

the party of the second part, to purchase said real property for the sum of   Dollars and reported said contract to the Court under oath as required by the said order.

AND WHEREAS by an order of said Court duly made and entered on the   day of   , 19 , the said contract and report were duly ratified and confirmed, and the said Special Guardian in behalf of the said infant was directed to execute, acknowledge and deliver a suitable conveyance of the said infant's interest and estate in the said property to the said party of the second part.

AND WHEREAS the said party of the second part has complied with all the terms of the said contract on his part to be performed,

NOW, THEREFORE, WITNESSETH that the said party of the first part, in consideration of the sum of
                                                            Dollars
paid by the party of the second part, the receipt whereof is hereby acknowledged, has bargained, sold, granted and released and by these presents does bargain, sell, grant and release unto the said party of the second part, his heirs and assigns forever, all that certain lot, piece or parcel of land situate, lying and being in the   , County of   and State of New York, and more particularly bounded and described as follows:

TOGETHER with all and singular the tenements, hereditaments and appurtenances thereunto belonging or otherwise appertaining and the reversion and reversions, remainder and remainders, rents, issues and profits thereof and all the estate, right, title, interest, property, possession, claim and demand whatsoever as well in law as in equity of said party of the first part of, in and to the above granted premises and every part and parcel thereof.

TO HAVE AND TO HOLD the above granted premises unto the said party of the second part, his heirs and assigns forever.

The grantor, in compliance with Section 13 of the Lien Law, covenants that the grantor will receive the consideration for this conveyance and will hold the right to receive such consideration as a trust fund to be applied first for the purpose of paying the cost of the improvement and that the grantor will apply the same first to the payment of the cost of the improvement before using any part of the total of the same for any other purpose.

IN WITNESS WHEREOF the said party of the first part, by his Special Guardian, has hereunto set his hand and seal the day and the year first above written.

In presence of

_____

_____ (L.S.)

By _____

Special Guardian.

Acknowledgement as
in form set out in D-7.

LAST WILL AND TESTAMENT

I, _____

being of sound and disposing mind and memory, and considering
the uncertainty of this life, do make, publish and declare this to
be my last Will and Testament as follows, hereby revoking all
other former Wills by me at any time made.

    First, after my lawful debts are paid, I give _____

I hereby appoint _____

_____ to be Execut_____ of

this my last Will and Testament.

    In Witness Whereof, I have hereunto subscribed my name,
and affixed my seal, the _____ day of _____ in the year one
thousand nine hundred and

                            _____ (L.S.)

                          Signature of Testator or
                                Testatrix

    Subscribed by _____ the Testat___ named in
the foregoing Will in the presence of each of us, and at the time

117

of making such subscription, the above Instrument was declared by the said Testat___ to be _____ last Will and Testament, and each of us, at the request of said Testat___ and in _____ presence and in the presence of each other, signed our names as witnesses thereto.

* _____ Residing at _____
        Signature

_____   _____
    Type or Print Name
_____ Residing at _____
        Signature

_____   _____
    Type or Print Name
_____ Residing at _____
        Signature

_____   _____
    Type or Print Name

*At least 2 witnesses required.

Affidavit of Subscribing Witnesses
                                    (Use of this Affidavit is optional)

STATE OF NEW YORK)
) ss:
COUNTY OF   )

On this _____ day of _____ , 19 ___ , personally appeared before me, a Notary Public in and for the County of _____ State of New York, _____
and _____
who being severally duly sworn on their respective oaths, depose and say that they witnessed the execution of the attained Will of _____

the within named Testator, on the _____ day of _____ , 19 ___ ; that said Testator, in their presence, subscribed said Will at the end thereof and at the time of making such subscription declared the instrument so subscribed by said Testator to be said Testator's Last Will and Testament; that they, at the request of said Testator and in said Testator's sight and presence and in the sight and presence of each other thereupon witnessed the execution of said Will by said Testator by subscribing their names as witnesses thereto; and that said Testator at the time of the execution of said Will, appeared to them of full age and of sound mind and memory and was in all respects competent to make a will and was not under any restraint; that they are making this affidavit at the request of the said Testator.

Severally subscribed and sworn
to before me this
day of   , 19

_____

_____

_____   _____

FORM OF ACKNOWLEDGEMENT (Individual)

State of   )
) ss.:
County of   )

    On the   day of   , nineteen hundred and
before me came .

to me known and known to me to be the individual   described in,
and who executed, the foregoing instrument, and acknowledged
to me that   he   executed the same.

FORM OF ACKNOWLEDGEMENT (Corporate)

State of   )   ss.:
County of   )

On the   day of   , nineteen hundred and
before me came   to me known, who,
being by me duly sworn, did dispose and say that   he resides at
No.

that   he is the   of

the corporation described in, and which executed the foregoing
instrument; that he knows the seal of said corporation; that the
seal affixed to said instrument is such corporate seal; that it was
so affixed by order of the board of
of said corporation and that   he signed h   name thereto by
like order.

INDEX

DATE DUE